PLANNING AND ORGANIZING PERSONAL AND PROFESSIONAL DEVELOPMENT

PLANNING AND ORGANIZING PERSONAL AND PROFESSIONAL DEVELOPMENT

CHRIS SANGSTER

Gower

Published by
Gower Publishing Limited
Gower House
Croft Road
Aldershot
Hampshire GU11 3HR
England

Gower
131 Main Street
Burlington
Vermont 05401
USA

Chris Sangster has asserted his right under the
Copyright, Designs and Patents Act 1988 to be identified as the
author of this work.

British Library Cataloguing in Publication Data

Sangster, Chris
 Planning and organizing personal and professional development
 1. Career development   2. Maturation (Psychology)
 3. Success in business   4. Self-actualization (Psychology)
 I. Title
 650.1

 ISBN 0 566 08264 0

Library of Congress Cataloging-in-Publication Data

Sangster, Chris.
 Planning and organizing personal and professional development/Chris
 Sangster.
  p. cm.
 Includes index.
 ISBN 0–566–08264–0
 1. Personnel management.

IIF5549.S1465 2000
658.3'124--dc21   00–021822

Phototypeset in 10 point Century Schoolbook by Intype London Ltd and
printed in Great Britain at the University Press, Cambridge.

CONTENTS

Preface   xi

I Setting your sights on the CPD goal   **1**

  1 What is CPD?   2
  2 Personal and professional: the difference   2
  3 Mixing and matching   3
  4 Personal and professional: the subdivision   3
  5 Individual empowerment   4
  6 Empowerment 'free flight'   4
  7 Some benefits of empowerment   5
  8 Making empowerment work   6
  9 Empowerment in context   7
10 The benefits of setting out a plan   8
11 The benefits of a systematic approach   9
12 The principle of 'triangular integration'   10
13 The integrated triangle   10

II Mapping your development path   **15**

14 The difference between training and learning development   16
15 Tracks and paths   18
16 The benefit of 'time outs'   19
17 The structure of objectives   19
18 Objectives: the facts   20
19 Psychomotor and cognitive objectives   20
20 Affective objectives   22
21 Cognitive objectives in detail   24
22 Advanced cognitive stages   27
23 An ongoing process   30
24 Business, departmental and individual objectives   30

25 Identifying stages   31
26 Milestoning   32
27 Modularization   33
28 Checking for hazards   34

III Getting your team together   **37**

29 Triangular integration in action   39
30 Motivating the manager   39
31 The support function in our triangle   41
32 Building the mentoring team   41
33 Setting lines of communication   43
34 Contracting to work together   45
35 Working and existing together co-operatively   45

IV Adding individual inputs to the team outcome   **49**

36 The holistic effect in detail   50
37 The holistic bonus   51
38 Involving line managers   51
39 Selling the benefits   52
40 Launching the concept of changing roles to DSF   53
41 Change begins to appear   55
42 Individual empowerment   55
43 Addressing strengths and shortfalls   56
44 Identifying needs   56
45 The outcome of the process   57
46 Eliminating the hidden agenda   59
47 Co-operation on a sliding scale   59
48 Planning and recording   61

V Moving along the development path   **63**

49 Preparing sound foundations   63
50 Setting off on individual development paths   64
51 The great time perspective   64
52 Goals and milestones   65
53 The Personal Pending file   66
54 Using a 'Things to Do' list   67
55 Personal planning   67
56 Personalized planner: suggested headings   69
57 A planning system   70
58 Monitoring progress   71
59 Prevention rather than cure   72
60 The power of communication   73

VI Learning along the way **75**

61 Reviewing the options 75
62 The hypothetical development challenge 76
63 Selecting from the range 76
64 Introducing objectivity into the selection 77
65 Selecting horses for courses 79
66 Overviewing the 'learning big picture' 80
67 Self-study 80
68 Open and distance learning 81
69 Training courses 83
70 Criteria for course type and technique evaluation 85
71 Coaching 87
72 Mentoring 87
73 The limitless scope of mentoring 88
74 Altering our perspective 89
75 The selection process 89
76 Viewing the big picture 90

VII Selecting the proper equipment **93**

77 Getting the correct combination 94
individual needs with training objectives 95
the strategy route 96
97
d solution 99
re detailed analysis 100
l conclusions 102
in the field 103
exibly to differing needs 104

VIII Charting progress **107**

purpose of progress 107
87 Why should we record CPD achievements? 109
88 Development testing for humans 109
89 Applying a CPD planning system 110
90 Plans, reality and lateral thinking 111
91 Problem solving to maintain progress 111
92 Triangular integration: is it working? 111
93 Using the CPD system constructively 113
94 Memo/discussion/action 113
95 Getting out of the mud 114
96 Using a CPD system positively 116
97 Our current position on the development track 117

IX Reviewing progress   119

98 Reviewing progress   119
99 Relating personal and professional development   120
100 The hundred monkeys   121
101 Spotting the signs of co-operation   122
102 Reviewing strengths and shortfalls   123
103 Establishing a review system   123
104 Using objectives to review progress   124
105 The range of objectives applied to the module   125
106 The real value of using objectives   127
107 Reviewing progress: Is the teamwork working?   127
108 Reviewing the foundations of our team building   128
109 Maintaining progress towards co-operation   130
110 Reviewing programmes and materials   132
111 Monitoring progress through competency testing   133
112 Reviewing the review process!   133

X Keeping our eye on the goal   135

113 CPD milestones   135
114 Planning an individual CPD project   136
115 Repositioning the milestones   137
116 Adding extra milestones to meet detailed needs   138
117 Case study   138
118 Spotting the potential blockages   141
119 Possible responses to meet identified needs   142
120 Charting the longer path, with added milestones   143
121 Negotiating to keep moving   145
122 Positive negotiation strategies   146
123 Keeping the pace going   147
124 The valuable new role of the DSF   148

XI Character building   151

125 Establishing our personal parameters   151
126 Focus on personal development   152
127 Personal development and the spiritual   152
128 Living a more holistic way of life   153
129 Holistic involvement in the community   154
130 Thinking and acting co-operatively   155
131 Co-operation within personal development   156
132 'Do me a favour'   157
133 The mentor over the garden fence   157
134 Personal development and the ego   158

135 The ego placed within a more selfless group dynamic 159
136 Selflessness and self-confidence: the positive self 159
137 Personal development and thinking objectively 160
138 Thinking in the active rather than the passive 161
139 Objectivity in personal development 162
140 Thinking objectively and impartially 162
141 Personal development and CPD planning and recording 163
142 Setting out our personal milestones 163
143 The ever-expanding state of personal development 164
144 Maintaining our individual momentum 165
145 Establishing the ground rules for a holistic life 165

XII Distant hills – charted paths **167**

146 CPD planning and recording 167
147 Reviewing the bigger picture 168
148 Reviewing our goals 169
149 Keeping an open mind 169
150 Empowerment – taking the lead willingly 171
151 Individual development paths 172
152 Integrating with others 172
153 Onwards and upwards 174

PREFACE

One of the benefits – and on occasion frustrations – of having been involved in training and development over many years, is that one experiences the full cycle of things reaching fruition (or not, as the case may be). Technologies and delivery media might alter but, in my opinion, the importance of objectively-formulated content remains paramount. It is not, for example, enough in itself that learning is delivered using interactive, virtual techniques. The most virtual experience will remain the real thing, if structured appropriately and overseen by someone with the neccessary knowledge, experience and patience. Which is where properly planned mentoring can have the edge over both formalized classroom training and the 'highest tec' delivery systems around.

This book represents the confluence of several streams of thought and experience which I have had over the years, leading to a belief that where a positive, mutually-supportive atmosphere can be created and (more importantly) sustained, self-development and empowerment can lead to a more holistic team outcome. The use of words such as *empowerment* and *holistic* may conjure up an 'other-worldly', brown lentil image in the eyes of some. I hope to demonstrate that they have a realistic and valuable application in the business world, albeit one which actually does respond to its mission statement of 'people being our most important asset'!

As a training consultant, I have had some of my most satisfying professional experiences working with positive-thinking clients who have seen the benefits of stepping back, re-assessing priorities and viewing the 'bigger picture' – that learning can be most effective when analysed and applied at the individual level. I advocate progression from the traditional matrix concept of seminar attendance towards the review of individual competencies, with personalized responses focused on addressing specific remedial shortfalls. This makes lifelong learning a positive experience where individual skills can be amalgamated within an active team atmosphere, culminating in more effective business outcomes. It also delivers an 'end result which is worth more than the sum of the parts', giving us the holistic paradigm in practice.

I have learned from too many people, situations, books and events to identify them individually. Life is truly a learning experience, if one remains aware of cause and effect. I would, however, like to single out for acknowledgement Colin Webb and Michael Milton for believing in me enough to help me climb the dividing fences between primary and tertiary education and between education and business training; Geoff Walker, Colin Cope and Harry Mitchell for seeing the professional benefits of 'bigger picture' thinking; Lyn Gladwin and Isabelle Kingston for making me more aware of this 'bigger picture'; Gillian Hill for both practical support and personal encouragement; and my wife Gillean . . . well, just for everything!

I hope that my enthusiasm for what I call 'triangular integration' transmits. If you would like to discuss the application further, please contact me through Gower or direct:

Chris Sangster
Ardochy House
Invergarry
PH35 4HR
Tel: 01809 511292
e-mail: ardochy@ukgateway.net

SETTING YOUR SIGHTS ON THE CPD GOAL

During my years involved in training and development, the challenge has remained the same: *to ensure that the content and outcomes are as applicable as possible to each learner's needs and that the learner then gets the appropriate opportunity and support to reinforce the new learning positively in the workplace.* The one should follow naturally from the other – but there are often hiccups.

I would also expect everyone to agree that *the benefits of training and development can only really succeed where actively supported by senior management.* And yet, if I'm honest, I would say there must be a relatively modest degree of long-term, direct senior management support for the implementation of development plans – and a frighteningly high percentage of information imparted to individuals under the general heading of 'training' that withers on the vine soon after the initial burst of enthusiasm.

There are many reasons why this may be so. Our role here is to think positively and to consider how we can encourage this enthusiasm, to facilitate continuing development. This must be as appropriate and applicable as possible, to be applied in the longer term. Current shareholder thinking often represents unacceptable short-term thinking.

The system which we will be considering involves a series of activities grouped around the generic process of Continuing Professional Development, or CPD. This process also incorporates necessary elements of personal development, which I envision as an individual development path through life. I have thus used the concept of a path and its exploration as the linking analogy throughout – I hope this aids understanding.

CPD MILESTONE 1 – WHAT IS CPD?

Under the heading 'What CPD is about', the Chartered Institute of Personnel and Development explains that 'the most important aspect of CPD is the outcome from the learning activity. Any activities in which new skills and knowledge are acquired and are then used in your career are sources of CPD.' Varied examples are cited, such as writing reports, mentoring others, being a Justice of the Peace, organizing sports events and attending courses and conferences – but there is no attempt to differentiate between *applications* and *outcomes*. Throughout this book, I will highlight this difference, and the distinction between *personal* and *professional* development.

CPD is an important element of both empowering individuals to take responsibility in their own development and assisting them, their managers and the Training Function to plan and record progress. Although some stances perhaps stress the *recording* element of CPD, I consider that the *planning* stage, directly involving the individual in objective thinking, is also all-important. Where monitoring and flexible review are incorporated, the recording of the outcomes becomes an automatic result of the overall process.

 ## CPD MILESTONE 2 – PERSONAL AND PROFESSIONAL: THE DIFFERENCE

As my involvement in training and development has evolved from management development and communication to personal development and personal management, I consider the differentiation between *professional* and *personal* development to be very important. It's evident that some learning outcomes – such as the structure and layout of a technical report or the application of a particular computer package – can be applied directly at the post-learning phase, while others, such as the skills relating to making objective judgments as a JP or organizing the logistics of a sporting event, need to be adapted fairly heavily to allow us to apply them directly in work.

Example

Some people are enthusiastic about team-building exercises that involve, for example, building oil-drum rafts to cross rivers, or similar physical challenges. However successful and enjoyable these may be in the field, they require major application and extended learning transfer for the outcomes to become valuable in the office. In the Co-operative Team Building course I run, I apply team-building exercises which use direct communication skills as the vehicle for the team-building debrief sessions. These outcomes can be applied more immediately within the workplace, because they are more directly relevant.

CPD MILESTONE 3 – MIXING AND MATCHING

We need a 'rounded' workforce – developed in practical skills and knowledge as well as in the social and interpersonal skills necessary to become an integrated member of the team. We no more want a computer specialist who, though a whizkid in IT matters, cannot have a meaningful discussion with others, than we desire an ex-military man who is *au fait* with leadership skills and the social graces but may be totally naive in business matters. Both personal *and* professional skills are necessary, as are the supreme efforts applied to mould them together to produce a dynamic end result. If we get this just right, we experience an holistic effect which is greater than the sum of the individual parts – this effect is a key objective of this book.

CPD MILESTONE 4 – PERSONAL AND PROFESSIONAL: THE SUBDIVISION

The workplace changed dramatically in the last decade prior to the new millennium, and this will undoubtedly continue. True, many scenarios reminiscent of Orwell's *1984* are only just beginning to reach realization, but examples of 'on-message, thought policing' and 'short-termism' are now appearing from some unexpected sources. Changing attitudes towards career development within a single, paternalistic company alter the corporate view towards the costs of intensive training and development; additional stress requires a more stable, balanced person to be capable of coping with work priorities.

Thus, learning and applying *personal* development skills such as objective reasoning, dynamic co-operation and stress management not only helps the individual cope with private and business life in a more rounded, confident way – but can also help when assimilating and applying particular *professional* development skills within the workplace.

CPD MILESTONE 5 – INDIVIDUAL EMPOWERMENT

Come to the edge, he said
They said: We are afraid
Come to the edge, he said.
They came.
He pushed them . . . and they flew.

Guillaume Apollinaire

As I apply the term 'empowerment', our involvement embraces assisting individuals to decide what they should do to develop positively; helping them to review these plans as necessary to maintain progress and providing the back-up support necessary to permit individual requirements to happen successfully. If we, as trainers or managers, provide this support and organization quietly in the background, we can take the individual's comment that 'they didn't do much – I arranged it all myself' as a compliment rather than a criticism!

Example

Over the years, I've run many 'Problem Solving and Decision Making' courses, and the difficulty with some client companies seemed to be establishing exactly what was meant by 'problem solving'. Many delegates were quite capable of logically reaching decisions – the challenge seemed to be that of second-guessing their boss's decision for a particular work situation. Empowerment can only enter a state of 'free flight' when the manager has provided a few criteria to assist decision making, while at the same time acknowledging that they will then fully support the individual's decision.

 ## CPD MILESTONE 6 – EMPOWERMENT 'FREE FLIGHT'

Empowering people to fly solo presupposes acceptance that, on occasion, they will fly off in a different direction from that expected by ground control – periodically, they may even plough into the trees. For empowerment to happen, we must fight the urge to keep control and 'do it ourselves'. Sit back, take a deep breath, remove your hand from the control column and let them fly.

There is some truth in the belief that people learn best when they have to figure things out for themselves. This 'figuring out' (within parameters which we establish, of course) encourages practical reinforcement, applied problem solving and direct involvement, resulting in a practitioner who has considered the 'hows' and 'whys' rather than trying to apply the instructions blindly, step by step.

Example

Remember those 'paint-by-numbers' pictures where you painted in all the sections marked 'yellow' and 'orange' and so on . . . and finished up with your Van Gogh 'Sunflowers'? You may have created a *completed* picture but the joins certainly showed – and you had learned little about composition and colour blending. These could only advance if you took the plunge and attempted to fly solo, on a blank canvas.

With ever-increasing controls for safety, legal and social reasons, there are, sadly, areas where we are in danger of being prevented from applying any degree of empowerment or self-discovery, with its implicit flexibility. Some training activities (such as safety training), which require the trainee to sign documentation on completion, appear to be carried out more to cover the company legally than to edify the learner developmentally. If we can think and act more openly, with a greater degree of co-operation, perhaps this 'ambulance-chasing' attitude towards compensation claims against employers will consolidate at a more sensible level, freeing up empowerment.

CPD MILESTONE 7 – SOME BENEFITS OF EMPOWERMENT

Consider the following:

○ An involved individual is a motivated individual.
○ A motivated individual can identify their development needs.
○ These needs require discussion – on an equal footing – with the individual's mentor.
○ The more specific the response to these needs, the more effective the learning.
○ Given appropriate application-support, individuals will reinforce their learning.
○ An empowered individual will identify ways of overcoming blockages.
○ An empowered individual should be allowed as much freedom as possible.

○   An empowered mistake is a heart-felt attempt which didn't quite work – this time!

○   An objectively-debriefed mistake will become a positive learning experience.

○   A supported, empowered individual will thus maintain high motivation.

It may be that you find it hard to accept some of the statements above. If so, that's not a problem – we're just starting out. As we progress, I hope that the benefits will become clear.

 ## CPD MILESTONE 8 – MAKING EMPOWERMENT WORK

As has been implied in the bullet points above, continuing empowerment needs a positive atmosphere, to be possible. This involves a wide range of elements, from senior management support to the availability of resources, from co-operative team spirit to accessible mentoring support, from effective communication to ongoing programme review. We will review these along the development path.

As we move along this path, we will hold periodic Route Reviews. These are designed to give food for thought and to check that arrangements are in place. As you become increasingly empowered, they will act as a prompt for developing a checklist of specifics which *you* will need to address, in order to facilitate the development of others – and of yourself.

As you haven't yet set off from base, you can take this Route Review as a practice. Consider each of these statements as they apply to you directly and respond accordingly by giving yourself a score on a scale of 1–10 (where 1 equals very little progress and 10 means that the activity/facility is already in place and functioning very well).

ROUTE REVIEW 1

1_____10
LOW   HIGH

■   It is quite an easy task in our organization/ company to subdivide between *professional* and *personal* development.

■   Time and money are equally available for

training in the 'soft' skills as in direct application, competency skills.

- Learning in many given subject areas can be achieved using a range of techniques and resources in our company.

- There is an effective communication system present within our organization/company, working in all directions.

- The general atmosphere is conducive towards individuals and teams being empowered to make reasoned decisions.

- The atmosphere in our department is such that empowerment can occur within a positive, supportive framework.

- Given such an atmosphere, there are several actions which I would like to carry out, which would improve effectiveness.

WHAT ACTIONS DO I NEED TO CARRY OUT?

 CPD MILESTONE 9 – EMPOWERMENT IN CONTEXT

Having a system and infrastructure in place is crucial to the long-term success of any development initiative. We don't pay good training and development money to change people's attitudes and competencies unless we are very sure that the facilities and resources will be available for the new skills to be applied long term. Yet I can think of many training initiatives which have had limited long-term success largely because the infrastructure necessary for the post-learning reinforcement was not properly in place, or was not maintained; for example, a single individual from a department is sent on a public team-building course, or delegates are trained on a system which is applied slightly differently within their own department/company. I'm sure you could add to this list from personal experience.

ONE STEP AT A TIME

Don't even think about applying empowerment until you have confidence in the infrastructure and support which is necessary for it to be given at least a fighting chance of success. Often, in training, you only get one chance to implement the outcomes. Rekindling an empowerment flame which has already been unsuccessfully attempted is very difficult – I have experienced this with reintroducing an appraisal scheme for a client.

Empowerment is the ongoing responsibility of the individual, but it usually needs quiet support and facilitation in the background. As a trainer or manager, this is where your involvement is important. Because the continuing professional development process involves everyone, the trainer or manager is also an individual with a personal CPD programme. It all becomes something of a continuum, with everyone 'reading off the same route map'.

CPD MILESTONE 10 – THE BENEFITS OF SETTING OUT A PLAN

You may have had some experience of map reading – I can certainly spend ages considering the implications of contours, river beds, alternative routes and possible road obstructions. In the Wiltshire area of southern England where I lived for several years, it was also fascinating to look at the ancient burial sites, standing stones and other signs of ancient pathways and try to imagine how lives developed and people interacted. The activities of CPD planning and recording are very similar to this map interpretation and route planning.

Consider the following:

○   CPD is a means of planning key development activities for the future.
○   Setting down logical flows helps us view the way ahead and predict potential blocks.
○   CPD planning makes us aware of alternative routes, improving our response time.
○   Having a CPD 'route map' encourages us to maintain a proactive view.

CPD MILESTONE 11 – THE BENEFITS OF A SYSTEMATIC APPROACH

We live in an age of documentation, presented evidence, desk-based assessments and so on – all mechanisms whereby we can check up on each other. Currently, more money and resources appear to be invested in *assessing* providers than in *supporting* the providers directly. Last year, for example, in the small primary school of which I was a board member, each teacher had around £300 to buy all classroom resources for the year, while a school inspector was paid well over £200 per day. Monitoring and assessment seem to be the growth industries of the moment, but this does not necessarily encourage empowerment.

VALUABLE APPLICATION

I believe that using a CPD system can be very beneficial, because it can have great value as a planning device: the monitoring process then becomes a direct record of confirmation. If we are advocating the planning and realization of development at an individual level, some form of individual record is crucial, to act as a specific reference point for the manager and trainer as well as the individual. As a former teacher, I know that it was impossible to recall the progress of my pupils without these reference records. Individual CPD documents are equally important and necessary.

Consider the following:

○ CPD permits achievements and progress to be recorded in a timely way.
○ CPD planning allows a view of the 'bigger picture'.
○ A CPD system encourages the dual focus on professional *and* personal development.
○ A focus on outcomes rather than activities permits a better chance of 'value-added'.
○ Individual CPD plans ensure that needs are analysed and responded to specifically.
○ A flexible approach to CPD planning encourages a regular review of priorities.

THINKING POSITIVELY

Continuing professional development documentation must not be allowed to become a deadening bureaucratic device – it must be a living, personalized planning and recording system, seen as valuable to the individual as well as to the employer. This system will represent individual needs and will respond to preferred learning and reinforcement strategies. It will act as a reference point during appraisal, encouraging a modular response to training/learning provision. These are some of the premises upon which this book is based: to encourage you the reader to think in this way is, if you will, my mission statement.

 ## CPD MILESTONE 12 – THE PRINCIPLE OF 'TRIANGULAR INTEGRATION'

I believe in the natural balance of three elements, best symbolized by an equilateral triangle. In the context here, our *integrated triangle* has the individual, the manager (or mentor) and the training support as the three corner points. In any triangle, the interaction of any two of these elements will have an effect on the third, and, in so doing, the three become interdependent. The relative energies expended by each will vary, resulting in an overall outcome for the individual which is far greater than the sum of the actual development activities listed in the CPD programme. I refer to this as the 'Holistic Effect' – it can equally be thought of as a dynamic synergy.

The integrated triangle is represented on page 11, with the training support identified as the '[development] support function', for reasons which will become clear.

We will be referring to this model extensively throughout the rest of the book, so let us take a moment now to define each corner.

 ## CPD MILESTONE 13 – THE INTEGRATED TRIANGLE

As the book is aimed primarily at trainers, let's start with your role.

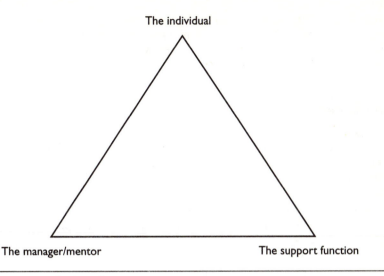

The integrated triangle

THE DEVELOPMENT SUPPORT FUNCTION

I am consciously using the title 'development support function', rather than 'training department'; to me, the name-change symbolizes a role-change, which may or may not be currently in place. In our triangle, we ask the manager to assume greater responsibility for supporting the individual's attempts at progressing their own development plans. We are also expecting the individual to take an active role in their own needs analysis and development. In order to facilitate this, the DSF must offer as much back-up and support as possible. A co-operative atmosphere is a must.

A fresh approach

If the DSF can provide a resources support role, this can respond to the needs of the individual in as flexible a way as possible. Some of these responses may continue to be placement of individuals on courses – nothing out of the ordinary there. However, there has been a fundamental shift away from the traditional activity of placing individuals on specific courses, to finding courses – or relevant modules of complete courses – which meet the specific needs of one or more individuals. Additionally, responses are equally likely to involve self-study, guided reading, open or distance learning, practical exercises and other routes, as well as mentoring by someone who has the necessary skills and/or knowledge. The DSF is thus acting as a resources bank stretching beyond the provision of workbooks, videos and inter-active computer programs to encompass resources in its widest definition. This will involve *any* support which can be used by the individual to attain their particular goal.

The revised role

The training department (in its revised role as the *development support function*) will have skills, resources and facilities which it can organize to support the needs of the individual and the mentor, facilitating learning provision *when required*. This calls for an aware-ness of the needs and the preferred forms of learning of specific individuals; a modular approach towards the provision and delivery of learning in its various forms – and a consciousness of the types of support which the managers/mentors will require.

Benefits for the DSF

A flexible, lateral-thinking approach is called for, which in some ways will involve additional work for the DSF. Initial work with the man-agers and mentors is required to build the atmosphere of co-operation, involving attitude, knowledge and techniques training as needed. However, this will result in a much broader base of 'trainers' to call upon (in the widest sense of the word, incorporating *ad hoc* mentors and coaches), more outcomes achieved informally and on-the-job, a higher degree of motivation for the individual learner, a more specific response to individual training needs, and a better guarantee of post-learning consolidation on-the-job and a more proactive atmosphere all round. As facilitators, DSF staff will be more involved in the design, evaluation and development of resources and the matching of these against specifically analysed individual needs. This seems an attrac-tive alternative to primarily delivering courses!

THE INDIVIDUAL

The individual is the learner, the trainee, the owner of any particular set of CPD plans and records. As, increasingly, each person in work (or aspiring to work) will use some form of CPD planning and recording system, having such documentation which focuses on the individual and their needs will ensure that the system remains a personal plan and record. We can all relate to this situation.

However, there is a slight complication. Because *everyone* is included in CPD planning, each member of the development support function and each manager or mentor will, in turn, become an individual learner when operating in that mode. Equally, I consider that anyone with a skill or knowledge to impart to another can assume the role of mentor (with a little initial training and assistance as required). So, by definition, a mentor will 'swap hats' and become an individual learner, while a staff member of the DSF can, at different times, be both a mentor or an individual learner. It is thus possible that you could at different times be represented by more than one of the corners of the triangle – and could be involved in all three roles. This should not be perceived as being a problem; indeed, it will perhaps help you see the situation from 'the other side of the fence', helping you to appreciate potential frustrations.

THE MANAGER/MENTOR

The manager/mentor is primarily the supervisor or manager responsible for the individual – and therefore involved in co-ordinating the CPD plans and relating them through appraisal with the business objectives of the company. It extends further than this, however. I consider a mentor to be anyone who has a skill or knowledge to impart to someone else. A mentor can be at any status level, as long as they possess the capacity to work with others in a sympathetic fashion. Many will require some level of training to help them design and deliver the information in a structured, sequential way, in digestible sections with appropriate reinforcement. However, we are not concerned here with higher-level presentation skills: the transfer of information will instead occur fairly informally, often one-to-one.

'Sitting with Nellie'

When training trainers in my youth, we used to speak of 'sitting with Nellie' in a rather off-hand, derogatory way. 'Nellie' was the employee who had been in the job for years and who took the new start under her wing. We trainers considered that she imparted bad habits, short-cuts and anarchy to the newcomer . . . the two must be kept apart at all costs! Having worked within many organizations now, I have come across some fantastic 'Nellies' (and 'Neils') who know the job and applications like the back of their hand and love the role of showing others. True, they need to be controlled and their enthusiasm channelled slightly and shown how to phase the information progressively and incorporate regular practical reinforcement . . . but these are your mentors. Use them positively.

Reversal of roles

You could thus have a manager mentoring a new inductee, fresh into the department on, for instance, safety and security matters, or departmental reporting policies. The same day, this inductee, who's highly computer-literate, could equally mentor the manager on spreadsheets, if the manager had an IT mental block in this area.

However, as a particular point of our triangle, we are perhaps more concerned with the role of manager/mentor as co-ordinator and reference contact, assisting in the development of the individual and the realization of their CPD plans.

Example

I worked with a client in writing and producing a complete induction and development programme for their customer service agents (CSAs), whose call-centre work involved product knowledge, fairly complex telephone and computer system operation and a wide range of problem-solving activities. To remove some of the pressure from the supervisors and managers, we developed a team of what we called 'Lead CSAs' who were invited (and volunteered) to act in the role of mentor. These were selected as having wide job experience, a sympathetic nature, an interest in imparting information and skills – and the ability to structure information effectively (after training).

Although some were more effective than others, this arrangement built up an impressive team of mentors who, as active CSAs in their own right, were on hand to assist individual learners. It did involve an initial outlay of time from the DSF to train them in the necessary skills, but this time was more than repaid in the first few months.

II

MAPPING YOUR DEVELOPMENT PATH

Before we consider mapping our development path, let's have a Health Check. This is necessary at each stage along the way, to make sure that we can all maintain the pace, pass the various milestones, and progress satisfactorily along the path.

HEALTH CHECK 1

Consider the following:

√   I can describe the difference between professional and personal development.

√   It may be possible for an atmosphere of individual empowerment to exist and grow within my working environment.

√   I can identify several benefits which I would gain personally, both for my own development and through supporting the development of others.

√   The potential for meaningful on-job reinforcement is there, where a proper support infrastructure can be provided.

√   I am aware of – and can discuss – the priorities of a CPD system.

√   I can describe the three roles involved in 'triangular integration' and can discuss how this integration can work flexibly.

√   In principle, I believe that I can accept the 'triangular integration' concept.

√   I support the idea that a CPD system requires both planning and recording.

DO I NEED TO DO ANYTHING TO CLARIFY THESE BEFORE ADVANCING?

I started my working life as a schoolteacher, with an enthusiastic interest in audio-visual equipment and resources and a desire for greater involvement with them. As a result of seeking out as much experience as possible, I landed a job as a lecturer in Educational Technology in London, working with teachers and Media Resource Officers. Here, I met my first mentor – or pair of mentors, actually. Although the department was based in a technical college and was primarily equipment-biased, the Head of Department, Colin, was an enlightened soul and advocated the benefits of a structured, objectives-based approach. I was placed under the wing of Gerry, who was also keenly enthusiastic, but he was most excited about composing objectives; he saw this as an academic exercise of creating perfect statements, without being too bothered about application.

REALIZING THE PURPOSE

Perhaps as a result of this, it took me at least eight years to realize the real practical benefits of using objectives, enabling a logical learning sequence to be designed for any particular programme – and to identify the most appropriate starting and consolidation points. This came through a study of the sequence of cognitive objectives (thanks to Benjamin Bloom's *Taxonomy of Cognitive Objectives*), which in intellectual terms basically shows you that you must crawl . . . before you walk . . . before you run – and that you need to reinforce each stage with lots of practice. Once the light of realization dawned, however, using objectives has turned out to be the most helpful skill I have ever achieved for designing and facilitating learning

 ## CPD MILESTONE 14 – THE DIFFERENCE BETWEEN TRAINING AND LEARNING DEVELOPMENT

We will look later at the range of techniques involved. At this stage, however, we want to concentrate on the potential outcomes that this range provides. First, is there a difference between training and learning development? The outcomes may be similar, applying comparable techniques but the emphasis is certainly different.

TRAINING

From my own experience as a trainer over the years, when delegates attend a training course, they often have few detailed expectations at the point of stepping into the room. They will be aware of the overall subject area and may have reviewed the course content or objectives against their own specific needs. Some may have discussed the objectives against business/departmental objectives with their manager. Delegates will, in the main, follow the course programme without questioning the content to any extent.

LEARNING DEVELOPMENT

On the other hand, we have learning development. When effective, learning development should incorporate motivation and empowerment on the part of the learner (while establishing *exactly* what their personal shortfalls really are) and two-way involvement between learner and manager to agree individual priorities.

This will result in a greater likelihood of there being opportunities to reinforce the learned information or processes. If the learner is directly involved at the needs identification/planning stages, they will be encouraged to think about priorities and applications – and can begin to identify the subject areas which they see as relevant to needs. If the learner's manager can spend some time talking this through with the learner *before* the learning event, it not only reinforces a heightened level of interest but also helps to underline the purpose and priorities of the learning outcomes. And (here comes our triangulation again), if the learner and the manager have taken the trouble to identify these needs and priorities before the event and they feed this information to the trainer as deliverer or facilitator, then the trainer must take it on board and react to it.

Example

I consider that this integrated involvement – our *integrated triangle* – is necessary to achieve both effective outcomes, and value for money. Let's say the going rate for attending a course is in the order of £350 per *day* (with hotel and travel expenses on top of that). Remember the school where each teacher has £300 to spend on resources for the *year*. To achieve 'added value', as the phrase goes, it's not enough for the learner to merely attend a course, even though the act of so doing will be noted on CPD record systems. The value to the learner is in assimilating information and skills which are directly relevant and *applicable* . . . and which bring added value to the organization. The importance lies in the *outcomes* of the event, not *attendance* alone.

SMART STRATEGIES

What is the strategy for mapping the learner's development path? The nub of the matter is to get the whole process as *specific* and *applicable* as possible. The development path involves parameters, that is, the outer boundaries beyond which the learner should not stray. These could relate to applications within the organization, cost, time involvement and other extremes which, if reached, should initiate a review process.

 CPD MILESTONE 15 – TRACKS AND PATHS

Visualize a long strip of land heading off into the distance, disappearing over the horizon as we view it. On either side of this strip is a boundary hedge. The strip could be as much as the width of a small field. This is the 'Long Straight Track' for every learner. As we are all learning, *your* development path will also run along this track.

One way to journey along the track is to take a line down the middle and go for it. But life's not like that. The track will include blockages: people will get in your way; a lack of resources or similar swampy patches will slow you down; time constraints will force you to detour and compromise rather than persevere endlessly. So, if you viewed from above, you would see this long straight track, with your path meandering progressively along it. Sometimes the learner will be surging forward in a straight line; sometimes curving from side to side to negotiate obstacles – on occasion, you may be static or even heading backwards. Overall, however, we should observe progress.

THE MERITS OF STANDING STILL

One of the confusing things all individuals must face when we take responsibility for our development path is the time element involved. This is symbolized by the meanders of the path along the track. Certainly, we can plan our route – the path – by using some of the techniques which we will consider. However, we often have little control over our speed of advance. This is a prime source of frustration, whether it is the youthful desire for rapid promotion, or, at a later stage in life, a more mature desire to improve things, based on experience. Instead of progressing, we sometimes appear to be standing still.

CPD MILESTONE 16 – THE BENEFIT OF 'TIME OUTS'

Patience, a clear focus and an ability to think laterally are all valuable attributes here. Standing still is not a problem – call it *consolidation*, *thinking time* or *reinforcement* and it becomes a distinct asset. As the pressures become tougher in work today, we need 'Time Outs' to recharge our batteries. This is *creative* or *lateral thinking time*, which is important to keep us both productive and fresh . . . and sane!

Consider the following, before you map your path:

○ It is important that co-operative agreement is reached before initiating plans.
○ Each individual may follow a unique path along the established developmental track.
○ Objectives and outcomes may be set, but learning techniques and methods are flexible.
○ Triangular integration is a responsive, proactive means of maintaining progress.
○ Time spent formulating the objectives before the journey is time saved during it.

CPD MILESTONE 17 – THE STRUCTURE OF OBJECTIVES

Most people have seen and worked with detailed objectives. These are called *behavioural* objectives because they point to an end activity or *action* – a change in behaviour which the learner will demonstrate an ability to achieve. The objective statement will also include an indication of the *standards* against which to measure the action or outcome, and any special *conditions* required to facilitate completion.

Example

You may have an objective for the activity of structuring a business report, for example:

> As an event outcome, the learner will be able (or competent) to structure the business report, incorporating the 'x' headings set out in the company's procedure manual, applying the prescribed sequence and utilizing agreed cross-referencing and numbering systems.

Notice that there is not a lot of clear water between objective and competency statements: an objective states an end activity which is measurable, while a stated competency confirms an ability to achieve a stated goal. I think that objectives tend to be defined more precisely – the key issue is the effectiveness rather than the title used.

 ## CPD MILESTONE 18 – OBJECTIVES: THE FACTS

Basically, there are three levels of objective:

○ Psychomotor: Practical, operational objectives, such as building something.
○ Cognitive: Knowledge objectives, such as the details of a procedure.
○ Affective: Attitudinal objectives, such as acceptance of a new system.

The example given above in CPD 17 is a (fairly advanced) *psychomotor* objective as it focused on the construction of the report following a set structure. An objective referring to the preferred content and style of the report detail would be at a *cognitive* level. An *affective* objective on this subject might be one establishing *why* structures vary between business and scientific reports, with an examination of their applications.

 ## CPD MILESTONE 19 – PSYCHOMOTOR AND COGNITIVE OBJECTIVES

It is easier to be specific with the psychomotor type of objective, because they usually contain concrete standards – numbers produced in a specified time, design specification to meet, volume, stated quality standards, and so on. With cognitive objectives, standards become slightly more generalized and thus harder to measure precisely. Following the same theme as before, a cognitive type of objective might state:

> As an event outcome, the learner will be able (or competent) to write a report which states the key recommendations clearly and precisely – and orders the supporting detail to reinforce each recommendation satisfactorily, presenting this as appendices where appropriate.

EVALUATING COGNITIVE OBJECTIVES

This evaluation is still quite precise but you'll note that it becomes slightly more subjective to judge. We'd need supplementary lists of criteria to check the report against – although this would not be a very difficult job to produce. What, for example, makes a recommendation 'clear and precise'? How do we cross-reference the information so that it clearly supports the recommendation? Establishing the standards or criteria becomes a more complex activity, but very necessary if we are to judge achievement.

THE OBJECTIVE AS FOUNDATION OF THE WHOLE PROCESS

When you have established these objectives, you have the foundations of our learning session and the basis of our standards. In situations where the learning method still relies on a human tutor or mentor, the flow of the session can be amended by the tutor in an *ad hoc* way, responding to any special needs or more detailed elaborations, to ensure detail transfer, that the standards are met . . . and the objective is thus achieved.

On the other hand, where we are using self-learn techniques, the design of the content will become more complex and detailed, as we must respond to possible areas which require greater elaboration or explanation. Achieving this, we can then help learners through identified misunderstandings or any other confusion which they may experience.

Writing clear and specific objectives as the initial point in the programme design helps to establish the criteria, the content, the sequence of development, and indeed the preferred techniques which can be applied to get the message over most successfully.

CPD MILESTONE 20 – AFFECTIVE OBJECTIVES

Affective objectives are the most difficult areas to consciously achieve set standards. In training and development, this process of change is often a fairly progressional thing rather than a blinding 'road to Damascus' type of revelation. It therefore becomes harder to measure the degree of overall success, especially when working with larger groups. To complete our trilogy, we could have the following as an affective objective:

> As an event outcome, the learner will be able (or competent) to discuss and implement the benefits of applying an established formal report structure throughout the entire organization, following stated criteria and format, in order to gain the benefits of standardization.

Notice that, although there is still a structure and criteria to work from, the key thrust of the objective is being able to convince everyone that the new, standardized way is best and must be applied universally. The purpose of the learning exercise therefore is to train people so that (a) *they* are convinced that the change is for the best and (b) they can then convince *others* that they too must change. Although the most obscure to achieve, we must sometimes address these affective issues initially, to alter attitudes and thus make learners more receptive towards the other structured learning objectives.

CONSOLIDATION

I trust that the examples have helped you identify the differences between the different forms of objective – and how they can be applied to develop the structure of a learning programme in a logical, progressional way. Basically, we can summarize these as follows:

Psychomotor objectives
- ○ Can set precise standards (quantity, quality, time and so on).
- ○ Can have the action stated in detail (as all psychomotor objectives involve 'doing').
- ○ Can be easily tested for achievement against the detailed criteria.

Cognitive objectives
- ○ Cover knowledge, understanding and application – it is more difficult to set absolute standards.
- ○ Consideration of these standards encourages better design of learning programmes.
- ○ This can lead to further subdivision, to give a 'scientific' progress to learning.

Affective objectives
- ○ Help to set targets for achievement, in terms of changed attitudes and beliefs.
- ○ Help to focus on the degree of success in effecting these changes.
- ○ Consideration of the various attitudes and blocks makes positive response easier.

Although traditionally, objectives tend to be thought of in the sequence above, I would end by reiterating that they are used flexibly as required, with attitudes addressed initially, knowledge and operational learning intermingled and so on.

You will probably be dealing primarily with *cognitive* objectives in your learning activities. Before moving further along our route, let's have a quick Route Review.

ROUTE REVIEW 2

1_____10
LOW   HIGH

■ My organization/company already uses objectives quite extensively, within training and at departmental level.

■ I can visualize the progress of a personal development path along a prescribed track of learning options and realize why this progress will be variable.

■ I can list and explain the three types of objectives and am aware of the difference between them.

■ I am competent at writing a psychomotor objective for an operational task, which includes action, standards and conditions.

■   I can see the benefit of being able to specify end
    actions which must be achieved, in order to chart
    progress.

ARE THERE ANY REMEDIAL ACTIONS WHICH I MUST CARRY
OUT?

 ## CPD MILESTONE 21 – COGNITIVE OBJECTIVES IN DETAIL

Benjamin Bloom's *Taxonomy of Cognitive Objectives* (Longman) gives
us a sequence for these objectives, starting at the bottom and progressing upwards as shown below.

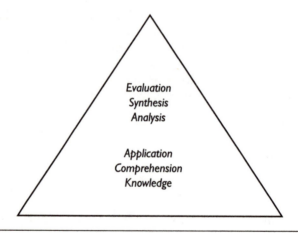

Learning development – the progression

Following behaviourist theory, this, in essence, gives us the sequence
of learning. (There are of course alternative theories but we'll stick
with this one for the moment.) Take a look at the different stages,
starting with the bottom three – knowledge, comprehension and application:

○   First, you must *know* the key items of information, names of
    parts, heading titles and so on. For example, know what the
    Control Key looks like and where it is located.
○   Then you must understand/*comprehend* what is actually meant
    by each part, heading and other key items of information, by

being able to describe the parts, explain their individual functions and generally show that you understand. For example, you would now have learned what the Control Key actually does.

○   The third stage is being able to *apply* your knowledge, perhaps in a practical exercise, or by discussing its overall application. For example, you could now use the Control Key to carry out the function you have described.

LEARNING AND REINFORCING IN 'DIGESTIBLE CHUNKS'

Often, this is as far as we can expect to progress during a training event, with the in-built practical exercises giving some experience of monitored application. At this stage, the trainer/mentor/facilitator must focus on ensuring that any learned knowledge is applied precisely as learned – it should be obvious that follow-up, work-based reinforcement is crucial, both to consolidate the learning and to lead to the higher levels.

Example

Let's practise this consolidation by reviewing an example: I've bought a new television, which has automatic tuning. I need to learn how to do this, so that I can tune in the various terrestial channels, to obtain a clear signal for each. (That's my objective – again an operational/ psychomotor one).

First, *knowledge:* I look at the manual and identify the appropriate controls in the diagrams – and relate these to the actual controls on the set and hand controller.

Next, *comprehension:* I need to delve a little deeper to find what the controls actually do, identify any particular fine tuning I need to do to get the best signal – and be clear about the sequence which must be completed to achieve the outcome.

Finally, *application:* with the set switched on and using the hand controller, I will follow the steps and stages (probably using a step-by-step checklist in the handbook) and actually attempt to programme the television. If it does not work first time, I will cycle back into the stages – perhaps initially following the checklist or going back to the explanatory sections to try to understand/comprehend better.

THE POSSIBILITY OF TAKING SHORT CUTS

You could argue that you could go straight to the checklist and work through the stages without knowing the functions of the controls – and still achieve the objective. This is true, although you would not necessarily understand *why* you were doing the actions. I would consider this to be another example of 'painting by numbers'. There's nothing wrong with this of course – take, for example, the emergency evacuation card which you find on aircraft: totally pictorial, step-by-step, with absolutely no explanations or descriptions, in other words pure application, for obvious reasons. Don't ask questions – just get off the plane by the shortest route. However, in setting up learning experiences, I believe that, if the learner understands *what* they are doing and *why* they are doing it, motivation is maintained in the longer term, which of course is not a consideration when evacuating from a blazing aircraft!

CONSOLIDATING THE LEARNING THROUGH RELEVANT REINFORCEMENT

So, knowledge, comprehension and application are the three lower echelons of cognitive learning theory. As I've already pointed out, additional reinforcement experience is vital at this stage. Over and above course exercises, supported on-the-job application is crucial. This is where mentoring can be very helpful – it's also where the development support function can actually support. You may think this is obvious and common sense. For example, we train someone to use a particular computer package because we need them to use it on a daily basis. They can apply their new skills immediately, with a little additional mentoring and coaching.

However, when you are involved in the cognitive and affective levels – especially in the areas termed 'soft skills' – the delegate can come back to the workplace and find it harder to experience direct applications. Take subject areas such as problem solving, counselling techniques, managing change or communication skills: it's hard to guarantee that some real examples for application will present themselves in those first crucial days and weeks after completion of the learning event, or that the examples which do occur can be practised following the stages exactly as learned. I consider it to be part of the role of the DSF or mentor as facilitator to make sure that such relevant experiences are arranged, so that the individual learner can benefit from the consolidation. It doesn't take a lot of effort – often just a quick word in the correct ear.

THE IMPORTANCE OF REINFORCEMENT

In learning, if you're reinforcing something, you're reinforcing it *exactly* as learned. It is important for mentors to realize this. The application stage is *not* where the learner is shown easy-do tips, shortcuts and other techniques which the experienced user/operator might apply. Any 'refinements' must be left until later, when the learner is capable of considering and making judgements regarding these alternatives to the established way. This will only come after several weeks, or even months, of practice ... which leads us neatly on to the three advanced stages of cognitive theory.

TIME OUT

It is important that you clearly understand the three 'foundation' stages of cognitive development, before you progress. Think it through for a moment before continuing – and perhaps read through the example again, to see how the progression works.

 ## CPD MILESTONE 22 – ADVANCED COGNITIVE STAGES

After – and only after – there has been an appropriate amount of consolidation and reinforcement of the principal skills, the learner will be ready to advance to the three higher levels – analysis, synthesis and evaluation.

ANALYSIS

When the learner is confident and well versed in the stages of the process, the details of the type of equipment, preferred layouts, procedures and so on, they can then use this knowledge and experience to *analyse* related or parallel examples. Thus, for example, you can use a problem-solving grid to identify the components of a particular problem by establishing how it subdivides and where the flaws lie.

Example

In a report-writing course, I might have spent some time establishing the actual structure of factual reports. I would have discussed, for example, the situation where there is a need for a table of contents, and where it should go. We would have considered the importance of having a section stating conclusions, or recommendations – and I would have underlined the importance of having this after the introduction, rather than at the end of the main report. Displaying a structure on the screen, I would have established the overall layout, the numbering system which we should use and the types of information which would be included as appendices. So, we would have worked through the stages of:

O   *Knowing* the component elements of the report structure;
O   *Comprehending* what was meant by each element; and
O   *Applying* our knowledge in discussing the basic layout of a report.

These, you will recall, are the first three cognitive stages which we have already covered. So, we would now be ready to advance to the *analysis* stage. As the name implies, I would produce one or two sample reports, written in full detail, and ask the learners to analyse them. In their analyses, they would be looking for the different sections as we have discussed them, checking for correct headings and numbering systems and whether the recommendations present the outcomes clearly.

When selecting these actual, written reports as examples, to what must I pay very close attention? Think for a moment . . .

I must make sure that they are 'good examples', which follow the structure I have been advocating and use the correct identification systems. Remember, this stage must give learners wide experience in *analysing* – *not* making valued judgements.

SYNTHESIS

Once the learner can confidently analyse examples, situations and behaviour against learned structures, knowledge and experience, further progress is possible. *Synthesis* involves the building up of component elements, based on previously learned knowledge and experience of parallel situations or matters. This is what your experienced car mechanic is applying to sort that annoying engine problem – or what a good, experienced manager is using to help staff apply procedures in real situations.

Example

Staying with our report-writing example, through analysing one or two reports, my learners have managed to consolidate the component elements of a report, what their normal logical sequence is, and the usual types of content which are included. In order to give them an opportunity to build up a report, I might now give them an exercise which involves reviewing a scenario or problem and structuring the outline for a report which would respond to this scenario/problem. So, at the end of the *synthesis* stage, the learners would have built up a structure to present and discuss, with the reinforcement being the activity of justifying their report design to the rest of the group.

EVALUATION

Once experienced in the intermediate heights of *analysis* and *synthesis* (operating at the levels of identifying, then assembling the logical sequencing of elements), the individual learner is ultimately ready to use these skills to make judgements and to identify sections of a process which are applicable in a particular situation.

Example

At this level, I might review the difference between factual and technical reports in order to make judgements as to the best structure for a technical report. We might identify, for example, that a table of contents is crucial for a technical report, but often superfluous for a factual one, or that the methods of investigation (or experimentation) must be provided in greater detail, to justify our recommendations in the report.

In *evaluation*, we are using information relating to a situation or system which we know to make judgements and present solutions for a parallel but new situation or system. Some people find this quite difficult, and it is often too high an expectation to have within a short training course. For example, some delegates on report writing courses which I have delivered do not want to consider alternative structures and scenarios, but merely want to be told 'the company way' of doing it. In some companies, there's a lot to be said for this approach, although it means settling at the application stage rather than entering into the higher levels of awareness or proficiency.

CPD MILESTONE 23 – AN ONGOING PROCESS

Applying evaluation is akin to climbing Everest – most of us will never really reach the summit. There are always lessons to be learned, better ways of doing something, amendments which must be made, and so on – but that's what makes life interesting, if you're willing to keep an open mind and see the bigger picture.

This has been a fairly brief examination of applied objectives – which represents a total way of thinking when related to learning.

Consider the following:

○   When planning, you begin to think in action statements.
○   When carrying out an activity, you think of ways of judging successful completion.
○   When working on a more complex project, you are aware of the logical steps and stages through which the project develops.

As should be clear by now, the process takes time to come to grips with – we will continue to apply it throughout this book.

CPD MILESTONE 24 – BUSINESS, DEPARTMENTAL AND INDIVIDUAL OBJECTIVES

We have touched on these during our review of objectives, but perhaps a more specific mention is required at this point. So far we have tended towards individual objectives, with perhaps a subdivision between personal and professional development.

PERSONAL AND INDIVIDUAL DEVELOPMENT OBJECTIVES

It may be difficult to apply some elements of your personal development directly within your company departmental role. This could be because some objectives relate to learned practical skills, such as a sport or a hobby, which are not directly applicable at work. It could equally be through work as chairperson of a committee, participation in voluntary work, involvement holistically with others in the community, society or other similar, personal goals. But there will be other individual objectives, which are required for your working effectiveness, such as learning new work-based skills, and interpersonal and communication techniques, all of which will make you a more effective departmental member.

These will often link with stated departmental and company business objectives; where personal objectives match departmental ones, this will permit the individual to begin identifying detailed content, and also to establish priorities. Thinking objectively (in the broader sense of the word), there is a distinct bonus in being able to apply personal attributes towards making our work performance better – as indeed there is in applying skills learned at work in our private life.

BUSINESS OBJECTIVES

Departmental objectives are a component element of the company's annual business objectives. All departments might share one or two common objectives (to increase market share by 5.5 per cent, for example), with individual departments having additional distinct objectives. These will usually involve sub-objective elements or 'building blocks' which, when added to those of other departments, will build towards the achievement of one or more major business objectives.

Thinking about how the various different objectives knit together in what I see as the *bigger picture* will certainly help you see how various developmental plans are formulated – and will explain why relative values mean that your manager may be keener to recommend your attendance on some of your identified learning needs programmes over others. It is sometimes hard to gain a view of this bigger picture, however – I have met many departmental managers who were quite vague about how their departmental objectives interfaced with those of others . . . or of the company.

 ## CPD MILESTONE 25 – IDENTIFYING STAGES

Let's look down on that 'long straight track' again. We will be focusing on the personal development path of one individual – although there will of course be lots of other personal development paths twisting and running along the same track. This could be the learning path of one of your reporting staff, or it could even be your own.

We know now that, because of blocks, delays and changes of mind and focus, the actual path taken by each learner will meander along the track, rather than heading along in a straight line. How might your own development path look?

Consider the following:

○ The development path will be a sequence of clearly stated objectives.
○ These can also be expressed as statements of competencies which must be achieved.
○ These statements will help establish milestone goals along the way.
○ 'Milestoning' is the action of ensuring the timely progress from goal to goal.
○ Personal progress and pace may be strongly influenced by business requirements.
○ *Controlled* and planned pressure at work can motivate positively.
○ Demotivation will occur when someone shifts milestones or causes major detours.

TIME OUT

The link between business and individual objectives is important – but it is sometimes quite difficult to see the interrelationship between the two. Try to think of – or find out – some of the key objectives which drive the work of your department or workplace; then establish some personal objectives which would help you participate in the achievement of these business objectives.

 ## CPD MILESTONE 26 – MILESTONING

'Milestoning' is a planning and monitoring device, which links directly with setting objectives and sub-objectives and is basically setting reference points along the planned development path, to monitor progress. It's not dreadfully scientific – visualize Dick Whittington making his way to London along a twisting road with periodic milestones where he and his cat rest to check the remaining miles.

Undoubtedly, milestoning helps us see the way ahead, and keep tabs on how we are progressing. Occasionally (because of our impromptu meanders to overcome obstacles and problems, or because of the need to get additional experience before proceeding), additional milestones may be added. The original milestone will still be there, however – it will just take us longer to reach it. Goals invariably take longer to reach than we intend. However, as long as we ultimately achieve our key personal milestones or goals, the timescale is often not very important. Having faith in our own abilities is important. Think positively, maintain a view of the bigger picture and be patient. We will be referring to milestones – and goals and objectives – consistently as we progress along the development path.

> *You will have wonderful surges forward.*
> *Then there must be a time of consolidating*
> *before the next forward surge.*
>
> *Accept this as part of the process*
> *and never become downhearted.*

Eileen Caddy, *The Dawn of Change*,
Findhorn Press, 1993

 ## CPD MILESTONE 27 – MODULARIZATION

Modularization sounds very grand – but is merely a way of thinking and planning. It is, however, a learning refinement that many people haven't thought about! Perhaps it's because it's harder to arrange for learners to only attend modules (or sections) of a course, requiring more thought at individual level. As the name implies, it involves subdividing a learning programme into modules, which happens naturally in Open Learning programmes, for example. This facilitates the selection of modules as appropriate to each learner. There are various reasons for subdividing a programme.

Consider the following:

○ Progressive modules tie in with our cognitive learning sequence (see earlier).
○ Some learners may only need to complete certain identified modules.
○ There may be a benefit in pausing between some modules, for practical experience.
○ Some modules may be relevant for use in more than one study programme.

○ Different techniques can be more easily applied to different modules.

○ Thinking in a modular way makes it easier to apply self-study methods.

○ Providing a range of modules permits learners to select preferred study methods.

We will consider modularization in greater detail as we progress along the development path – it is certainly a key step which is a first sure indicator of a move from traditional training department thinking, towards assuming the role of a development support function. It indicates a focus on the learner's as well as the department's needs.

 ## CPD MILESTONE 28 – CHECKING FOR HAZARDS

If you've ever dabbled with Advanced Motoring, you may have heard the term 'defensive driving'. One element of defensive driving is checking the route well ahead, to be forewarned about any potential hazards. Often, a slight release on the accelerator will allow the potential hazard to sort itself out before you reach it – result: non-existent hazard.

This is a good technique to use in problem solving – spend some time thinking of the range of potential blocks and delays which might happen. For each, think through some possible release strategies which might help move things forward again. Look out for problems developing and respond, using the enlightenment you have achieved from your previous hypothetical planning. It's viewing life as the big picture again!

Consider the following potential hazards to someone's developmental learning, perhaps your own. Try to think of five additional hazards which you have experienced:

○ Learning time is cancelled because your services are required due to short-staffing.

○ There is no budget to send you on a specified external training course.

○ Accessing equipment for practical reinforcement will be a problem.

○ Your identified mentor is too busy to give you the support you need.

○   You are too important to be released for two complete days of training.

○   Your domestic situation makes it difficult for you to attend residential courses.

○   There is nobody in your department who is expert enough to mentor subject 'x'.

○   The training department does not think the need is a priority (your manager does).

○   Your manager does not think the need is a priority (the training department does).

○   Your motivation has slipped because of some bad previous learning experiences.

Checking for hazards prepares us for the different eventualities, however, and puts us in a stronger position to find alternative routes round the obstacle, negotiate for an acceptable compromise and generally identify ways of keeping our developmental path moving forwards positively. We will review hazards as we progress further.

GETTING YOUR TEAM TOGETHER

Before we move on, let's first check our progress.

ROUTE REVIEW 3

1————10
LOW   HIGH

■ Using objectives is an integral part of the business life of the company where I work at the moment.

■ Using objectives in a more informed, sequential way will help me work and live in a more focused, confident manner.

■ A more flexible approach to responding to individual learning needs will allow a more precise, motivating response.

■ Business/mission statements, annual and individual objectives and departmental priorities all make the parameters of the company's developmental track clear for all to see.

■ As an individual, I am in the position where I can analyse, synthesize and evaluate company processes and priorities.

■   It may be possible to modularize development programmes to a greater extent, to allow greater learning flexibility.

IS THERE ANYTHING I CAN DO TO CONTINUE MY PROGRESS?

We need to put energy into developing our teams, although, as previously mentioned, I favour more business-related strategies. However we do it, we need to develop a real bond between the different parties. Like an expedition of mountaineers roped together, our team bond must be one of complete trust. What are some of the criteria for this complete trust required by the mountaineers?

Consider the following:

○   Individual members will be proficient – and will maintain standards at all time.
○   There are no 'prima donnas' – all team members work for a common objective.
○   Individuals will maintain lines of communication between each other at all times.
○   The team will motivate each other but will normally move at the pace of the slowest.
○   Each individual is responsible for the equipment used and for its maintenance.
○   Each individual will use this equipment correctly, in a controlled manner.
○   Each individual will bring their skills to the expedition, for its overall benefit.

I could go on, but hopefully the picture is beginning to emerge – there's not a great distance between a team going up the North Face of the Eiger and a team of people working together for a common end, in business or in private life. On the rock face, the sportsfield, the stage or in the workplace, there's nothing to beat the buzz you get from being part of a team which is pulling together successfully towards a common goal.

THE HOLISTIC PRINCIPLE

The final criterion above introduces another concept which will be a recurring theme in this book: the concept of doing things for the common good, which I refer to as the 'Holistic Principle', also referred to as 'altruism' and 'selflessness'. It may be difficult to achieve at times, especially when we are involved in a highly assertive work environment, but I believe that the overall benefits will slowly make themselves apparent. We will consider this principle and the real role and position of assertiveness within the co-operation hierarchy further, as we progress through the book.

 ## CPD MILESTONE 29 – TRIANGULAR INTEGRATION IN ACTION

Co-operation is important if we want our learner/manager/support function triangle to work effectively. Look at the mountaineers' criteria again – that's how we want our triangular integration to work: fluidly and seamlessly.

Here's something to try. Find a rubber band and, holding the thumb and first two fingers of one hand pointing towards you, place the band round your three fingers to form a triangle. The tops of your fingers represent the three parties in our integration. Move your fingers around, sometimes with the three close together, sometimes with two, sometimes with the three spread out, functioning separately. That's the way integration should work – with varying degrees of interaction, but always conscious of the existence of the other parties. If one finger slips out of the rubber band, you have two fingers advancing and retreating from each other – the fluidity has gone.

 ## CPD MILESTONE 30 – MOTIVATING THE MANAGER

We have already set out the roles of the three parties – here we are more concerned with seeing the payback for involvement in these roles, or the 'What's in it for *me*?' question. Sounds a bit selfish but we're all human, even managers. The sad thing is that many managers were promoted because they were good at *doing activities*; then they become managers and spend their time at their desk or in meetings, *talking* about others doing these same activities: salesperson to sales manager, classroom teacher to head of department, carpenter to clerk of works, even adult to parent. Many managers will welcome the opportunity for involvement in the development process.

SELLING THE IDEA

It shouldn't be too hard to sell the benefits of this involvement to managers, as the result will be a more motivated departmental member (our individual learner).

Consider the following:

○ Being involved with individual members of staff will keep your finger on the pulse.
○ It will give you first-hand involvement with current processes and problems.
○ Getting feedback about details of the business will help your own planning.
○ Being actively involved will save you getting piles from sitting around too much!
○ Motivated staff are more likely to work *with* you, as part of the department team.
○ Active discussion will make the appraisal process more dynamic and meaningful.

If they think about it, they probably have some good ideas to apply, as long as they can count on help from the DSF. They may even enjoy the involvement, if they get the DSF's backing – it's all part of the idea of co-operation.

Example

Recently, I worked on a six-month contract in the procurement department of an engineering/manufacturing company. Two operations managers were recruited latterly who were genuinely keen on building up the expertise, empowerment and team spirit of their workforce – I and several others had the role of being the support function. It was an inspiration working with them, although by the end of the project, sheer pressure of work brought about by the popularity of the end engineering product (coupled with production problems and some knee-jerk management reactions) meant that they could not devote the necessary time to the development of their staff. Going back to our rubber-band analogy, we (as the support function 'finger') latterly drew closer to the individual learners, with the manager 'finger' pulling further away.

The communication and team dynamic in our triangle was still there, however, and there was definite progression down individual development paths. One solution to the managers' restricted availability was to identify mentors from departmental members with greater experience. With appropriate training, they did this very successfully.

CPD MILESTONE 31 – THE SUPPORT FUNCTION IN OUR TRIANGLE

Responses to individual learning needs are best provided from a range of techniques, including short and longer courses, self-study, open and distance learning, mentoring and coaching, practical project work and others. We will review these later.

The flexibility of some of these (especially the non-training course events) means that many of the developmental learning responses can take place informally on a daily basis. This must be a key benefit! It does, however, mean that the support function must initially produce or procure the learning modules which will be used directly by the learner or as support resources for the mentor. This gives a subtle change in role for trainers, from being primarily deliverers, towards both providing resources and working with internal mentors and coaches to develop their skills. This is another major benefit.

CPD MILESTONE 32 – BUILDING THE MENTORING TEAM

After identification and appropriate training, having this body of mentors and coaches ready to help in the face-to-face development and reinforcement will also be a key benefit. True, the initial training will be time-consuming, but as a result of this preparatory work, the support function can build a wonderful network of real practitioners. These mentors will maintain an up-to-the-minute awareness of the current needs of both the department and individual learners. Our concept of triangular integration will help line managers and support function managers to 'read from the same route map', thereby allowing the overall development track to be planned to meet as wide a range of needs as possible.

PROVIDING INDIVIDUAL RESPONSES

Meeting individual needs in a modular and timely fashion is a greater challenge than merely providing a menu of set courses: a la carte rather than table d'hote – and even then, allowing for the possibility that some may move straight from starter to sweet, or merely select parts of the main course. The development stages of setting up a resources bank, and then the maintenance of these resources, are quite hard work. But once the materials are on the shelf and the programmes are running flexibly, it relieves the pressure in the longer term, when we step back and look at the bigger picture.

Example

Several years ago, I was approached by the European training manager of one of the largest international courier companies. At the initial point of contact, he was 'thinking course delivery' – his problem was that, on any given Monday morning, he could have new customer services agents requiring induction training in multiple control centres in any one of the eleven different countries, for which he held responsibility. And only he and one other assistant were available to provide the training courses!

As our conversations developed round internal mentors/'buddies', on-line practical training, support materials, manager/supervisor involvement and other elements building towards a self-contained modular approach to the problem, the overall solution became one which could be used in all work sites, utilizing local facilitation. As well as training the mentors, we also familiarized supervisors in the programme's use and brought the key managers together centrally to experience the finished programme and 'buy in' to the benefits. It was hard work, as all the concepts were new, but well worth it.

The role of the training department thus evolved dynamically to provide development support, supplying resources (such as training videos and replacement specialist materials), monitoring progress, evaluating outcomes and maintaining a team of mentors and supportive managers/supervisors. In short, it became a support function, providing a very valuable, flexible service, without requiring day-to-day involvement in direct training and delivery:

Problem → Solution → Empowerment.

◼ CPD MILESTONE 33 – SETTING LINES OF COMMUNICATION

To return to the rubber band analogy: it's a flexible means of linking our three points together, thus allowing freedom and independent movement while at the same time providing support and balance where required. That's what *communication* should give us.

Consider the following:

- ○ Many interrelationship problems can be traced to breakdowns in communication.
- ○ Communication is at least a two-way process – otherwise, it's dictatorship.
- ○ There is a benefit in setting down/confirming agreed outcomes in *writing*.
- ○ There is a benefit in face-to-face communication, where negotiation is involved.
- ○ E-mail communications must not be used as a cowardly way of dodging discussion.
- ○ In a three-way relationship, two-way communications should consider the third party.
- ○ Communication benefits from milestones – allowing agreement of stage-outcomes.
- ○ Apply the maxim 'if in doubt, try talking about it.'

Example

When I was International Training Manager for an American airline catering company, I was involved with employees right across the board. One day, I might be running a kitchen hygiene event for shop-floor operatives – to them, the Supervisors were the problem; another day, running a programme for the Supervisors, they saw each other as working closely as a team ... but the Manager was the problem. Speaking to Managers, they were doing their best to carry out the whims of an ever-changing flow of resident country VIPs and so on. Although there were plenty of mission statements and edicts issued, there wasn't a vast amount of two-way communication.

IF IN DOUBT – TRY TALKING ABOUT IT

Poor communication, in different manners and guises, has duplicated itself in many of the client companies I have worked with as a consultant. Although many companies may have complex communication strategies and technologies in place, communication at the very basic level of face-to-face talking and listening is often inadequate. Poor communication leads to demotivation, wasted time and the distinct possibility of duplicated efforts – which leads me on to the benefits of working co-operatively. But before we do this, let's have a Route Review.

ROUTE REVIEW 4

```
1_____10
LOW    HIGH
```

■ There is a potential atmosphere within my company (or group of colleagues) where a team spirit can grow positively.

■ I can think of certain individuals who might have a harder problem integrating into the team – and I know why.

■ I can think of a situation at work or elsewhere where a co-operative atmosphere has helped the outcome of an activity.

■ It will be possible for managers to support their staff in the development of learning activities.

■ Our Training Department has the will and resources to shift its emphasis to become more of a Development Support Function.

■ I can think of at least five ways in which my Company – or Department – could improve its range and quality of communication.

■ I can list five techniques which I could personally apply in order to maintain better links and communication with those around me.

HOW CAN I MAKE THESE THINGS HAPPEN NOW?

CPD MILESTONE 34 – CONTRACTING TO WORK TOGETHER

We've already considered co-operation, which is an important element of the holistic way of life. Take a football match: you will have seen a piece of set play developing, with the ball passed, players positioning themselves to receive the ball and the striker finally blasting it into the top corner, well clear of the goalkeeper. Although the striker is obviously nominated as the actual goal scorer, the entire group of players involved get a favourable mention. All work together as a team.

CPD MILESTONE 35 – WORKING AND EXISTING TOGETHER CO-OPERATIVELY

There are three stages in the progression towards working as a closely-knit team, whether this is climbing our rock face, playing in a team, working in our office or liaising within any group of people. Picture the situation when you join a company.

BELONGING

Belonging is the initial stage. You're excited about starting work. There's a novelty in having your new desk and work station (where company policy permits). You've had your induction, so you now know the building layout, the company's mission statement and what your pension rights are when you retire. You've got some work to do so that you feel you're adding something to the company – but you aren't threatened by your work demands. You feel comfortable – you belong. Depending on the individual, this feeling can continue for some time. Some people may even be quite happy to remain at the Belonging level, and they become the office or workplace stalwart.

ASSERTION

However, once the feet have settled under the desk for a while, most people begin to crave slightly more recognition, through greater involvement and responsibility. Being more aware of those around them, they become more confident about their own skills and capabilities – and wish to publicize and apply these more. This is the second, middle stage – that of *assertion* (or *assertiveness*, as it is often called). But take note: this is the middle stage, *not* the ultimate goal.

Assertion as a positive attribute

Taken positively as a natural progression, the art of assertion is one of selling your own attributes, showing others what you are capable of and actively seeking opportunities to apply your skills positively. Some people find it difficult to do this, due perhaps to a lack of confidence, hesitant communication or not wishing to 'push themselves forward'. This concern at raising heads above the parapet is quite understandable.

The 'tall poppy' effect

You may have heard of the 'tall poppy' effect – it is prevalent Japanese business practice, and there is a fair amount of it in the British business psyche as well. It refers to the situation where a taller poppy head is likely to get trimmed so that its stem height conforms with the other heads (losing, of course, its own head in the process). This is applied, in a fairly heavy-handed way on occasion, in some environments. In that atmosphere, it's not a good idea to be seen to know more than the boss – any ideas of applying mentoring arrangements in such an atmosphere would have to be applied in a strictly hierarchical, 'grandfather' manner. I support neither inflexible mentoring nor 'tall poppy' thinking, which often has hidden, personal agendas.

If we view assertion as a middle stage, heading towards *co-operation*, we begin to see assertion in a different, more positive light. Assertiveness training should have the objective of permitting someone who has stuck at the 'belonging' level to project their attributes more positively and confidently. This will encourage that person to promote their skills and competencies co-operatively within the team or department.

CO-OPERATION

It must be acknowledged that the shift from assertive to co-operative thinking is a very difficult one for some companies – and individuals – to make. Picture the scenario: you have certain skills which you have found the opportunity to develop and apply, as do I and others in the Department where we all work. Perhaps you and I are both fairly expert at a particular skill, so we have to sort out whether one of us is responsible for it, or whether we can share involvement in some way.

These various skills will then go into the central 'pot' of competencies which the Departmental Manager can deploy in order to make the outcomes and outputs of the Department as effective as possible. Moving towards this level of co-operation helps develop team spirit, and promotes the positive atmosphere of 'reading off the same route map', which we have already mentioned.

Example

When training groups to give group presentations, I stress the importance of working co-operatively at all times.

While working as a senior consultant with a major London training company we had the unwritten rule that we supported each other publicly *at all times*. We did not correct colleagues in front of course delegates, even if they made mistakes; we came to their support if they showed signs of drying up or getting their resources in a mess, and we would support each other and the company if, as occasionally happened on residential courses, delegates ganged up against one of the tutors.

When you are working in a group, knowing that you can rely on this level of support and co-operation from colleagues is a great boost to confidence – and it is something which I would want to instil in every presentation group I work with. Everyone has strengths and shortfalls – the beauty of working co-operatively in a group is that you can build members' various strengths together holistically to give an enhanced overall effect, while at the same time minimizing or compensating for individual shortfalls. A holistic team evolves, with no 'passengers' being carried.

As with the applied benefits of the cognitive process, I believe that this three-stage co-operative progress is a very useful model. As we continue along the development path, we will revisit its advantages in helping us work together . . . and holistically.

ADDING INDIVIDUAL INPUTS TO THE TEAM OUTCOME

Before we progress further, let's pause for a quick Health Check.

HEALTH CHECK 2

Take some time to think about each of the points below:

- √ I can now see assertiveness as a stage in the overall co-operative process.
- √ I can think of skills which I and colleagues can use better and more positively in the department (or other form of team environment).
- √ I can name four ways in which communication could be improved for the team.
- √ I can identify three skills at which I would like to be more proficient.
- √ I can describe how triangular integration can work within my own work environment.
- √ I can discuss two concerns I have regarding potential teamwork.
- √ I can describe workable solutions to these concerns – and my involvement in them.
- √ I can identify those skills which I could bring to a group project.
- √ I would enjoy working as part of an integrated team.
- √ I can think of situations where I have experienced group synergy.
- √ I understand the similarities between this and 'the holistic effect'.

TIME OUT

Take a little time to think about the quote below:

We are members of a vast cosmic orchestra,
in which each living instrument is essential to the
complementary and harmonious playing of the whole.

J. Allen Boone, *Kinship with All Life,*
Harper and Row, 1954

Being a member of an orchestra is a rather nice analogy –
perhaps an even better one is that, as members of a team,
we are like jazz musicians 'jamming' in a club. Each one of
us gets the opportunity to show our virtuosity in at least
one solo spot, before returning to become one of the backing
band, driving the music along.

CPD MILESTONE 36 – THE HOLISTIC EFFECT IN DETAIL

Grouping together individual skills to form a composite outcome gives
that extra 'secret ingredient' – the jazz band's inspiring, tight-knit
sound, for example. This is what the holistic effect is all about. The
effect will be present when we begin to apply co-operation effectively.
Through (positive) assertion, individuals in any team will establish
the skills which they consider to be valuable and applicable – many
of these skills will complement each other, producing a more dynamic
end result.

Example

Let's take an example which I apply in an event entitled 'Communicating towards Co-operation'. I have already mentioned the exercise
of giving a team presentation. Let's say that in this particular group,
there are four members – Andrew, Brenda, Chris and David. Andrew
is not very keen on public speaking but he is a wizard with Powerpoint.
He's also very good at using and explaining the technology and equipment side of things. Brenda has a very professional-sounding voice
and gives a very polished presentation. However, she's a little inexperi-
enced, and doesn't like handling complex questions. Chris is good at

writing – and has had lots of experience in the subject. She can produce effective case studies for the practical workshop and write the presentation notes. David has had many years of experience with the subject and has an extra 'gravitas' which will be valuable for keeping the presentation moving forward positively.

Each person has individual skills. Ask them to produce four individual presentations on the chosen subject area and each presentation would be effective in some aspects but potentially weak in others. Combine them in a team presentation, with co-operation from initial planning to final delivery and reinforcement – and you have a winner.

David could chair the team, introducing the topic and team members, before handing over to Brenda to give the main presentation. This would be supported by the visuals produced by Andrew, who would also ensure that the technical side of the presentation flowed seamlessly. After consolidating, Brenda would hand over to Chris to run the practical exercise (using the prepared materials) and David would round off by leading the question and answer session, involving the others. The result is a holistic synergy.

CPD MILESTONE 37 – THE HOLISTIC BONUS

It's this add-on bonus, so to speak, which is the benefit of the Holistic Effect. At its simplest level, it's the sheer excitement which comes about when a group of individuals is working together harmoniously. It expands further where individual skills or competencies flourish through being placed together. This is evidently a benefit for the individual as well as for the group outcome. It works in music – and in business as well.

We have considered triangular integration and how individuals work productively with each other – now we should consider each individual component in greater detail.

CPD MILESTONE 38 – INVOLVING LINE MANAGERS

I don't think I've seen a job description for a management position which doesn't include 'training and development of reporting staff' in the list of responsibilities. And I've come across many managers who were enthusiastic about training their staff. But, however keen the manager is in becoming involved in training initiatives, we must acknowledge that training is only one managerial responsibility. Many more responsibilities require a more immediate response – often as higher priority issues. When 'push comes to shove', the immediate requirement must be to keep the business running. Sometimes, with' the best will in the world, managers just cannot afford the time (or sometimes staff) to become involved in training to the degree they may wish.

This is a fact of business life which both the individual and the DSF must accept if the atmosphere of co-operation is to be allowed to grow. Understandably, we all think that our work is the engine by which the company runs and the overall outcome is achieved – but there is a sliding scale of importance, if we're honest.

GETTING THE PRIORITIES RIGHT

Training and development ensures that staff are capable of delivering efficiently and effectively . . . but there is a progressive line of priority here. We often lose track of direct causes and effects in business. Training or administration processes should always be designed to suit company needs and priorities – that is the whole point in training needs analysis (TNA). However, how many of us have occasionally had to amend our priorities and methods of work to fit in with rigid administrative or organizational methods? Is, for example, voice mail always a real benefit to the *customer*?

 ## CPD MILESTONE 39 – SELLING THE BENEFITS

So, if we are to encourage line managers to become directly involved in the training and development process, we must first convince them of the benefits. We must be able to demonstrate that their needs and priorities are being listened and responded to – and that they will be able to organize the learning events within their line department.

Consider the following:

O   Direct involvement will ensure that needs are met as specifically as possible.
O   Involvement prior to any training and development (T&D) will raise awareness.

○ Knowledge of the T&D content will permit more relevant reinforcement.

○ T&D provided on-site will reduce the need for staff to be absent for periods.

○ Manager and supervisor involvement will raise the atmosphere of motivation.

○ Direct involvement will ensure phased practical reinforcement, post-training.

○ Modular support, using material provided by the Support Function, will be seen as a cost-effective method of response.

○ Involvement in identifying priorities and content will encourage management 'buy-in'.

THE DSF's ROLE AND ATTITUDE

The achievement of much of this will be the responsibility of the development support function (DSF). The ease of achieving it will, to some degree, depend on the current role, mind-set and openness to change prevalent in the training department, which may currently be run in a fairly conventional manner. There can sometimes be a slight air of suspicion, mistrust or disillusionment between line and training departments. The training department must launch its new development support function image positively to the line managers, because it may only get one chance.

CPD MILESTONE 40 – LAUNCHING THE CONCEPT OF CHANGING ROLES TO DSF

You're clear about the milestone then – there it is, with 'New DSF Role' written on it, standing slightly further along the track. That's your goal: to reach that milestone and bring all (or at least the majority) of the line managers along with you. How can you achieve this goal, selling the concept of change to becoming a Support Function? You'll also want to clarify your new responsibilities – and your new relationships. This can be accomplished by:

○ selecting a subject area about which you feel confident – both in terms of your own knowledge and a belief that it can work within the chosen environment;

○ initially working on a small, manageable project, which has clear objectives;

○ choosing to work with a line department which you know to be supportive;

○ working closely with the line manager, providing maximum support possible;

○ procuring and/or producing the necessary resources and programmes in a timely fashion, in order to respond to new requirements as effectively as possible;

○ ensuring that line department personnel are capable of using all the materials and programmes provided, to ensure optimum results;

○ providing any internal department coaching/training necessary, relating to any techniques (e.g. mentoring) which are required for successful project achievement;

○ facilitating the activities within the line department (perhaps to a greater degree than you would chose to do normally) to ensure that progress is maintained;

○ applying the 'defensive planning' we spoke of earlier, to pre-empt problems and get alternative strategies in place to maintain development and achievement;

○ reviewing progress regularly and communicating this and successful outcomes; and

○ using this initial success as a reference point when talking to managers from other departments, in order to line up the next department(s) keen on being involved.

I didn't say it was easy! The first attempt is the hardest, partially because it's new to everyone. There might even be the remnants of suspicion around: 'What's the training department trying to do – passing the buck and asking us to train our staff? That's *their* job.'

TIME OUT

Before moving forward, consider as many of these suggestions above as you can, in the context of *you* applying them within *your* organization. Which departmental/line manager would be most amenable? What subject area would work well in that department? How would you go about building up the support materials? Go on, give it a try!

CPD MILESTONE 41 – CHANGE BEGINS TO APPEAR

When you see this application of the triangular integration concept in real-life situations I hope you can see some of the potential. I've used the strategy on several occasions and it does work – when the spirit of co-operation begins to kick in, you have a true sense of dynamic achievement, of something happening which is bigger than the sum of the separate activities put together. The crucial element is the selection of a positive-thinking line manager who is keen on the overall concept of training and development, and eager to sort out a *significant* operational problem.

The indication of the breakthrough point, when you are beginning to succeed, is when the manager of line department 'B' complains that you are focusing too much effort in department 'A' and asks when you are going to come and support development in Department 'B'. Now you can positively negotiate terms for involvement.

KEEPING UP WITH THE ENTHUSIASM

Of course, there is a danger that the Support Function can become the victim of its own success, as more departments want you to provide a support role for their particular departmental development programmes. At this point, your next programme should be one which can be more widely applied, potentially keeping more learners (and line managers) happy as a result of the same design and development effort.

 ## CPD MILESTONE 42 – INDIVIDUAL EMPOWERMENT

In our earlier example of group presentations, we selected the natural capabilities (or competencies) of the individuals and built them together to give a seamlessly professional presentation. In other situations, you may have skills requirements within your department which are not currently met by any of the department's members. Or you may have new policies or processes which the majority of the staff need to learn. There are different situations and needs . . . but the general principle is always the same.

CPD MILESTONE 43 – ADDRESSING STRENGTHS AND SHORTFALLS

We can't be uniformly good at everything: it's natural to have shortfall areas. It's what we *do* about them that's important. We must all think of shortfalls in an open way – our own as well as those of others. We are not in the game of trying to disguise or hide particular shortfall(s) – instead, we will look them square in the eye. At this point, we perhaps need to subdivide – between those which we feel we can improve, and those which we will never be confident or competent at applying.

Example

In order to write this book, I've used my word processor package quite confidently and can produce visuals, documents and brochure masters for my workshops and other activities – which is the extent of my requirements. I've also produced computer-based and interactive video programs. But I move rapidly outside my comfort zone when people start elaborating on advanced techniques.

In a way, this is one of my shortfalls – but I don't currently need these advanced techniques so it's not a shortfall I wish to pursue. I have other shortfalls which I am capable of improving, and will develop further in the future. I can shelve the lower priorities as they are not important for my current or perceived forthcoming activities.

 ## CPS MILESTONE 44 – IDENTIFYING NEEDS

When I facilitate self-development events, one of the first activities which I ask individuals to do is to list their strengths and shortfalls. Strangely enough – call it modesty or whatever – many people can specify their shortfalls more easily and rapidly than their strengths. Perhaps it's because others have identified their shortfall areas!

Example

Imagine that you are the individual learner being considered, and try to develop your personal list. Note down your five key strengths and your five main areas of shortfall. Don't think too hard – just let the ideas flow and note them down.

When you have done this, look at your identified shortfalls and, against each, write a brief strategy of how you could improve your performance. Remember, you don't necessarily need to develop each to the point of being a strength – you may however need to get it to a point where it is not hindering your work – or life, for that matter.

If, in all honesty, you feel that you really cannot improve your performance in a particular shortfall, put a cross against it. If you finish with more than two crosses against your five shortfalls, you might be becoming vulnerable – so review them again!

ANALYSING INDIVIDUAL STRENGTHS

Strengths are not a problem – it's a question of degree. Some will be considered to be satisfactory at the level at which the individual currently operates; the performance of others might benefit from an even higher competency, through additional development. These development strategies should be reasonably clear – often, they amount to ensuring that the individual gets wider and more advanced practice, with perhaps some mentor support. Sometimes, of course, the additional development will involve a more formalized learning of advanced techniques or supplementary processes.

 ## CPD MILESTONE 45 – THE OUTCOME OF THE PROCESS

Where each individual is empowered to consider their own strengths and shortfalls, as well as potential development strategies and work-related priorities, this will usually increase the motivation level. The process can also make the individual a more active participant during appraisals and development needs analysis, even advancing to the point where the individual becomes virtually an equal participant with the other two representatives of the integrated triangle – the manager and the DSF.

SHORTFALLS

It helps if you consider individual strengths and shortfalls – and particularly the shortfalls which the individual may find it difficult to improve to any marked extent – within the context of the holistic team concept. You will see that some of these individual shortfalls will become immaterial when reviewed within the amassed capabilities of the total team. The department can then mix and match individual capabilities quite flexibly, presupposing, of course, that *everyone* has *some* strengths (or even improvable shortfall areas) – otherwise we are entering the unwanted realms of passenger carrying.

THE INITIAL STAGES OF 'SETTING FREE'

There are some people who will probably always require some degree of control and who will find it very difficult to become personally empowered; by the same token, there are some who regard self-study as a chance to do very little. These individuals will require closer monitoring, management and supervision and will need to be directed to a greater extent. Some will respond and be set free.

It's time for another Route Review.

ROUTE REVIEW 5

```
                                                         1_____10
                                                         LOW    HIGH
```

■   I understand how individual skills can be integrated within the team's overall competency levels, for improved outcomes.

■   The atmosphere could be developed within my company, department or peer group to allow the holistic effect to happen.

■   I am currently, or could be involved in activities where holistic team activities could be applied beneficially.

■   I can identify and discuss a strategy that the training department could apply in order to change roles to provide more of a Support Function for individual and team development.

■   I can identify my own strengths and shortfalls, relate these to my work and/or life role and plan an outline development strategy.

■ There is a particular work-related activity area in our department which would benefit from a more advanced teamwork approach.

WHAT CAN I DO TO MAKE THESE THINGS HAPPEN SOON?

CPD MILESTONE 46 – ELIMINATING THE HIDDEN AGENDA

There's nothing more lethal to a growing sense of empowerment, motivation and positive enthusiasm than hidden agendas. We've all come across them:

○ Younger applicants being preferred ... in order to potentially reduce salary costs.
○ Company 're-engineering', invariably resulting in redundancies.
○ Deferred regulations, which come into force some time after initial announcement.
○ 'Signed-off' training, implemented primarily to cover the company legally.
○ Training needs shortfall discussion considered a 'black mark' against the individual.
○ An individual's transfer of skills to others, which is then abused by making that individual redundant.
○ Open discussion during appraisal subsequently used negatively against the appraisee.

You've probably had personal experience of several others. As we've considered earlier, when you experience someone working independently at a highly assertive level, out for personal gain at all costs, the hidden agendas can appear quite frequently. If we have aggressive competition directly challenging a more co-operative stance, the competitive outlook will invariably win – to some large degree because the parameters for having 'won' are different when viewed from the two aspects.

CPD MILESTONE 47 – CO-OPERATION ON A SLIDING SCALE

Let's revisit the subtler applications of assertion/co-operation interactions. We have previously established that co-operation is a progressive step beyond assertion. At this greater degree of refinement, the 'rules of engagement' are slightly different when a co-operative person is dealing with someone who refuses to progress beyond assertion.

Example

Let's say that a co-operative person ('C') wants the assertive person ('A') to compromise for the overall good of the team – to pass the ball to someone who is in a better position to score, for example, or to hand over research notes to someone else, so that they can add the detail to their own knowledge to solve a customer problem. 'A' will see 'C''s compromising attitude as weakness, and will tend towards refusing to collaborate. In order for the impasse to be broken, 'C' will have to regress to an assertive stance – facing up, speaking forcefully, removing the item or debating the case confidently with 'A'.

It took me some time (and a few situations where I 'lost' the argument) to realize the need to do this – looking from a higher, co-operative viewpoint, it seems wrong to have to, in effect, lower your standards. But I now acknowledge that it sometimes becomes necessary to do this for overall progress. Keep giving in (as seen from the assertive perspective) and you will soon be considered to be a 'soft touch'. Stand up for your principles – say 'no', even – and people will have to reassess your interrelationship.

KEEPING THE MOMENTUM GOING

Thus, eliminating hidden agendas and getting people to read off the same route map are two key issues which you must address positively for personal and team development to be allowed to progress. Problems associated with these two concerns will undoubtedly constitute some of the blocks which will cause delays and detours on our learners' development paths along the track. However, being aware of them and considering alternative strategies will help keep individual learners ultimately on course.

At this stage, a brief review of planning strategies is required, in order to underscore their importance for maintaining the momentum of the individual development paths.

CPD MILESTONE 48 – PLANNING AND RECORDING

As we've already established, various techniques (such as specifying objectives, milestoning and identifying strengths and shortfalls) can be applied to planning individual continuing professional development (CPD) strategies. At this stage in our journey, I would like to introduce a few ideas for you to reflect upon as we progress.

Consider the questions below, as they would apply to someone reviewing their future CPD planning (the questions would of course apply equally in the situation where you were considering your *own* development plans):

O   What additional areas of information do I require to be able to work effectively?
O   Where or to whom would I go to find out this information?
O   How can I prepare beforehand to ensure that I am clear of my objectives?
O   How can I best store/manage this information for future reference?
O   Which additional skills/competencies do I require to maintain progress?
O   What different learning programmes are available for me to use?
O   Which type of programme would I find most motivating?
O   Would I prefer the programme to be organized, informal, flexible or a combination?
O   Is it possible to subdivide any learning programme into modules?
O   Do I see some modules as being more important than others?
O   Would it be possible to be selective in choosing and phasing these modules?
O   How specific can I be about my shortfall areas relating to these modules?
O   How do I find out about formal training courses which might be appropriate?
O   Can I identify specific programmes which match my personal priorities well?
O   Are there internal mentors/coaches/trainers who can help me informally?
O   How do I identify these – and what procedures would we follow?
O   How do I prioritize my development needs and goals?
O   How can I best monitor their progress?

We need not be too concerned about the detail of these at the moment. Try to view it all as a bigger picture, as an overall view of development planning. As you will appreciate, there is quite a lot to take on board. However, many of the stages progress quite naturally, when we think about them within context. The questions represent a logical planning sequence which I have used successfully to help many people structure their future development, so they're certainly worth a little consideration.

Half the fun of getting there
is the adventure we have along the way.

MOVING ALONG THE DEVELOPMENT PATH

Let's focus on the track again. You may be thinking that, up to this point in the book, your path hasn't progressed much. However, look back at our Contents pages and you'll see the milestones we've covered. We have been focusing on planning, building the atmosphere for positive team interactions, setting the parameters for triangular integration and looking at some of the criteria required for individual empowerment. In other words, we've been getting our foundations right first.

 ## CPD MILESTONE 49 – PREPARING SOUND FOUNDATIONS

To establish good foundations, planning and preparation are crucial. This is as true for building or construction work as it is for self-development. It took me many attempts at house painting to realize that the improved finish achieved by the professional painter was largely due to the initial preparatory work – the rubbing down, the filling and, above all, the undercoating, in order to prevent drips in the dried paintwork. Preparation is also needed for producing sound development programmes.

We are now ready to progress towards the longer-term, bigger picture. The foundations we have already laid include addressing personal empowerment, establishing the roles in triangular integration, applying development objectives, reviewing the benefits of co-operative team working – all of these building towards a holistic effect as a result of developed individual strengths and shortfalls.

Now we can focus on the individual.

CPD MILESTONE 50 – SETTING OFF ON INDIVIDUAL DEVELOPMENT PATHS

It may be worth acknowledging at this point that we are viewing the path in a multi-faceted way, linked closely overall with our concept of triangular integration. Our key thrust is the examination of how the DSF can develop the overall function in order to respond to individual priorities. However, members of the Support Function team can at times be personally acting as mentor to some individual. At other times, they can of course be individuals in their own right, involved in their own CPD.

SOMETIMES THE LEARNER, SOMETIMES THE FACILITATOR

At times, therefore, you may see yourself as the individual recipient, at others, the facilitator. This is not a problem – indeed, it should help you see the strategies, activities and priorities in a more realistic way. It should also permit you to relate more closely to the selection of methods of realization for each individual – including yourself.

A CLOSER VIEW OF THE WAY AHEAD

Accompany me to the point on your development path which we have reached so far. Perhaps you feel that there's still a long way to go. In 'life-long learning', there certainly is – but you know that the overall track has now got sound foundations. There will be fewer potholes and marshy areas to fall into – and a greater possibility of keeping away from some of the thorny outer limits of the track's constraints. Also, now that the foundations are laid, we will be able to progress faster.

> *Begin with the possible; begin with one step.*
> *There is always a limit, you cannot do more than you can.*
> *If you try to do too much, you will do nothing.*

> P.D. Ouspensky and G.I. Gurdjieff

CPD MILESTONE 51 – THE GREAT TIME PERSPECTIVE

Though there will be meanders and blockages along your path, there is always a way forward. It may not necessarily be the way you had planned – notice that, so far, our planning has been to ease the way forward, not specify your series of milestones in vast detail. Also, we must realize and accept that the total timescale is the element over which we have least control. Maintain your end focus, however, and it will happen, ultimately.

When I was about fourteen, my ambition was to be a shepherd and own a Land Rover. My parents thought differently and I finished up qualifying as a teacher. As I write this almost forty years later, with various areas of education and training experience behind me, I will shortly be moving to Scotland, with sheep and Land Rover. One of my own personal development goals will be achieved – even with a forty-year incubation time!

Perhaps we can accept longer periods of waiting for personal goals than professional ones – I certainly wouldn't have waited forty years for major promotion. Indeed, I progressed from school teacher through lecturer, adviser, training centre manager to senior training consultant all within a period of seven years: different drives give different degrees of impetus. We certainly can achieve ultimate control over our way forward.

CPD MILESTONE 52 – GOALS AND MILESTONES

We have mentioned the 'bigger picture'; that is, the benefit of looking at things as an overview and seeing it within an overall context. This is equally true when considering development plans. Traditionally, we tend to focus on the training course which we will attend in two months, or the part-time qualification we're progressing towards achieving in a year or so. This can cloud our vision of longer-term and wider development, and indeed *why* we are involved in particular areas of development.

Each individual should consider and review this Individual Development Checklist periodically:

○ You are aware of your personal strengths and shortfalls.
○ You can order these in terms of your own sequence of priorities.
○ You can review this sequence against your work priorities, as you understand them.
○ Your work priorities can be clarified through appraisal and informal discussions.
○ You will also be aware of some/all of the major goals you have in life.

○ Combining these thoughts, you can begin to identify milestones along the way.

○ Some of these goals will relate closely with each other – others will be separate.

○ You should begin to see the high priority goals, both for work and life in general.

○ Thinking laterally, sometimes you can progress towards a goal indirectly.

○ Review your progress regularly and flexibly – use your Personal Pending file.

 ## CPD MILESTONE 53 – THE PERSONAL PENDING FILE

What's the difference between a paper in your In tray and one in your Pending tray? Simple: if it's in the In tray, you haven't done anything about it yet; if it's in the Pending tray, you've considered the content and tried to advance but, for some reason, you can't progress further at the moment. It's the same with goals and milestones.

There are times in work and life when progress on a particular issue becomes stuck: you hit an operational problem, the manager is not there to OK some action, the required equipment is not available – the list is endless. You can sit there staring the problem in the face – or you can put that goal on hold in your mental or physical Pending tray and focus your attention on another one. By the time you've progressed the second goal along the track a little, the problems blocking the first one may have eased, or might even have resolved themselves and disappeared.

Example

For a short spell, I worked with a company involved in producing CBT programs, designing and producing an interactive video program for one client. The director became stressed when I had to 'pend' the project while waiting for periodic script reviews. This was largely because there were no other projects to work with, creating non-productive periods. In my own business, with several projects running in parallel, it becomes a matter of scheduling the work – you probably do the same with the various items on your 'Things to Do' list.

CPD MILESTONE 54 – USING A 'THINGS TO DO' LIST

You must have a 'Things to Do' list, whether it is an elaborately printed 'Activities Prioritizer' or just a basic blank sheet of paper.

KEEPING THE BRAIN IN GEAR

Writing lists, whether they be linear or branched ('mapped') to relate associated ideas together, is a very good way of overview planning, as well as helping to set priorities. At the other end of the process, being able to tick off completed items gives a wonderful sense of achievement – a simple but effective form of motivation! Refresh and update priorities by writing a replacement list periodically, which helps identify blocks.

CPD MILESTONE 55 – PERSONAL PLANNING

The ground rules of CPD suggest that we must register our plans and record their realization – with perhaps slightly more emphasis on the recording than on the planning. From our present position in our journey, these viewpoints are represented by the personal development plan and the learning/development log. There are various products on the market which assist in producing and maintaining these records – both paper- and IT-based. I don't think that the complexity of technology really matters, as long as the recording system is easy to complete, consult and update – and can be applied flexibly.

ESTABLISHING A SYSTEM

If the individual is clear about what they want and the techniques for bringing it about, all that is required is a sheet of paper and a pencil. We need some consistency and organization for the entries, of course – some people will be happy to control this themselves, while others will prefer tried and tested structures. What we certainly do not want in any system is too many prompts, headings and guidelines, which can hinder rather than help. Users of any system must actually think about the format options available and only use those which are helpful, to the extent which they are helpful to them personally. If it is felt that completing particular sections for a specific area of need gives little 'added value' to ongoing development, time should not be wasted completing it. It is better that the focus is on the sections which *do* have a valid point and where detailed response to the various headings is helpful.

TIME OUT

Before you read any further, try this as a practical exercise in planning your progress.

If you were asked to set down a series of headings for the sections of a CPD Planning system which would help *you* plan your individual goals (and milestones towards each goal), what would you chose to include? Ask yourself which headings you would find useful as prompts when planning both your personal and your professional continuing development, to allow greater consistency over the longer term. Make a note of these headings on a sheet of paper.

When you have finished, compare your ideas against my list of suggestions below in CPD Milestone 56. This might help you add or subtract one or two and perhaps refine the content of some.

DEVELOPING YOUR PERSONALIZED CPD PLANNING AND RECORDING SYSTEM

After any final refinements and revisions, set your ideas out as a list of headings which you would include in your personalized planner. Remember, the key purpose of these headings is to prompt you to respond consistently. The degree – and indeed the relevance – of the responses will vary, dependent on the actual subject area and degree of applicability. Also remember that, although these headings may suit your needs, other individuals may have different priorities. We're thus hoping to develop a system flexible enough to allow it to be used by different individuals.

Be aware that each individual may subsequently be using the planner as a reference point for discussion with (probably) their manager during appraisals and other forms of progress review. These discussions will feature the personal priorities listed by the individual, but will also incorporate those priorities which are specific to the individual's department and any annual business objectives identified by the company.

REACHING COMPROMISE

Thus, thinking co-operatively, the final list of future activities which result from discussions at appraisal will be a consolidated compromise of these different priorities. Some of the individual's personal selections may have little relevance to the company's business objectives and might therefore remain in the pending tray. This may ultimately have to be accepted graciously. Perhaps next year, priorities will have shifted!

 ## CPD MILESTONE 56 – PERSONALIZED PLANNER: SUGGESTED HEADINGS

I would find most of the following headings useful:

- My personal development goals.
- Subdivided milestones of how I might progress with these.
- My professional development goals.
- Subdivided milestones of how I might progress with these.
- Areas of information shortfall.
- Possible sources of gaining further information.
- Areas of competency shortfall.
- Possible activities to improve these/alternative strategies to overcome them.
- Prioritized target areas.
- My key priority needs areas set down as objective statements.
- Indications of where I might find formal training responses to these needs.
- Indications of where I might find informal/internal responses to these needs.
- Some indication of the responses which are more possible to activate.
- Some form of overall development plan, with milestones, to chart progress.

There's quite a lot there, but don't be put off. Even though my system might include a sheet for each of these headings, I would still apply them selectively. If a system becomes too much of a chore to complete, the 'documentation time' will eat into the development time – and we're back into the administration calling the shots again.

For this reason, any planning system must be seen as a servant, not a master. Only use sections as and when they prove to be helpful. If the individual is clear *why* there is little point in completing a certain section for a particular planning need – there is no point in completing it. Use the time more productively, on priority needs.

 ## CPD MILESTONE 57 – A PLANNING SYSTEM

If you do not have the time or inclination to develop your own personal system, or would prefer one based on general CPD principles which can be used fairly flexibly within your organization, there are several systems available. The Chartered Institute of Personnel and Development has a computerized system available to members (call 020 8971 9000 for further details); my company produced an individual development planning system in 1988, which I have further revised recently to form the basis of a forthcoming system of checklists.

Whatever system you consider using, the detail required in the individual sheets should be fairly self-evident, if you apply the headings as we have been discussing. Use any system as flexibly as you wish, rather than inhibiting yourself by trying to follow overly rigid structures and rules which are implied or stated. Remember, any system is there to support the individual, who should never distort priorities or content to suit a structure which is not one hundred per cent relevant. It should be used selectively and consciously – and be amended as necessary to suit specific needs.

When working with others to complete and apply our system, for example, I always suggest that some formats are more applicable to personal than to professional development – while others may apply to practical rather than knowledge outcomes (and vice versa). It's a case of formulating elements of your development path clearly in your mind and then applying the most appropriate format to document them.

RECORDING PROGRESS

The other side of the coin – recording progress – is much simpler. It happens as a natural development, if the individual has organized the planning clearly. The headings, priorities, milestones and expected time-frames in the 'x'-month development plan will already be set down. With direct reference to this, the individual can see what should be happening (in overall and specific, milestone terms), when it should have been completed and whether these stages have been completed on schedule.

CPD MILESTONE 58 – MONITORING PROGRESS

We've already established that the final schedule of personal goals for the year will be an amalgamation of some of the individual's personal priorities combined with key business priorities as stated in the company's business objectives. In terms of formal development events, therefore, the individual may not have been given the authority necessary to attend some course or courses which they've personally identified as being crucial for development. If the individual thinks laterally, however, it may well be possible to spend some time informally with an internal mentor – someone who is already competent in the skill considered to be an area of shortfall – in order to develop it further. It may also be possible to receive subsequent guided practice and experience.

There are different ways of achieving an objective – don't take refusal as a personal slight, as there are always limits to the funding and time availability for development activities within any organization.

Monitoring progress becomes much easier for anyone – including you – if you've done the planning and set it down in writing. If priority needs, stated goals and objectives and projected milestones indicate how you expect the development path *should* progress, with identified strategies of how these various steps and stages might be achieved, it then becomes an easier job to check how the development path has *actually* progressed. Any mismatch indicates blockages on the track, at which point your lateral-thinking, problem-solving approach is activated to formulate alternative strategies.

> *A confident hand on the tiller*
> *and an accurate chart of the shoals and channels*
> *will ensure steady progress through the stormiest of seas.*

The rate of progress can be affected by a very wide range of influences, some of which we will have greater control over than others. Having clear plans helps us remain as objective as possible when identifying any blocks – and any possible solutions.

 ## CPD MILESTONE 59 – PREVENTION RATHER THAN CURE

Regular monitoring of the established plans gives us as much prior warning of potential hazards as possible – remember our defensive driving in CPD Milestone 28. We're looking here at what is often referred to as 'fire prevention' rather than 'fire fighting'. When providing a supporting role, this could be the simple act of ordering something in plenty of time so that it is available at or before the point when it is required. Forward planning is an integral part of monitoring progress. Time spent on preparing foundations and arranging logistics will be more than saved through smooth and steady progress.

SEEKING HELP

It's one of the golden rules in climbing that, before you head off into the mountains, you always advise somebody about your intended route and expected time of return. Then, if you do get lost, rather than blundering around in the dark, you settle down in a tent, survival bag or snow hole and wait to be rescued, blowing your whistle periodically. True, you've inconvenienced many people but they won't mind too much as long as you've behaved in a professional manner and not tried personal heroics (which might result in you being carried injured off the mountain, or worse).

Heading out on your development path is very similar to climbing that mountain. As long as individuals behave in a professional, co-operative manner, people will usually help them, often preferring to get involved before or at the point when they are beginning to be lost, rather than having to drop everything and rush to the rescue. A key area experiencing many problems is where communication is not applied properly.

CPD MILESTONE 60 – THE POWER OF COMMUNICATION

Communication is a basic competency which we can all achieve if only we keep its importance uppermost in our minds. Key skills include presenting detail at the identified level of understanding of the listener, listening and responding to questions and replies, consolidating periodically to ensure clarity and understanding – and agreeing on outcomes/actions before closing the discussion of the topic.

Note the importance of listening – communication is always a two-way process. Most of my preferred strategies are still founded on a belief in the distinct benefits of real human interactions. This can be face-to-face, over the telephone, even by video-conferencing – but there will always be, in my mind, intrinsic benefits in live, immediate interactions as opposed to the likes of e-mail or impersonal memoranda. Sometimes it is necessary to initially set down reference details, recommendations, priorities and so on as the basis for – or registering the result of – discussions. But the related face-to-face interactions will drive the progress. All simple and straightforward, if you think about it. But *do* think about it – and discuss the implications with others. There is so much talked *about* communication but rather a limited amount done *with* it.

GETTING THE CO-OPERATION FLOWING

At the point where we have some degree of co-operative involvement and our triangular integration is working, there should be plenty of sources of help to call upon. And if the atmosphere of mentoring, coaching and other informal means of working together is in place, help (as they say) should be 'just around the corner'.

Part of the ethos of empowerment, of course, is self-help. If the individual can problem-solve objectively, is aware of possible and alternative strategies and is informed about the support resources which are available, then they can seek help personally from within, as well as from others. It's not as odd as it sounds.

Often, we have access to the solution, directly or indirectly, if we ask the right questions. This is one of the key differences between mentoring and coaching: coaching is built on the acceptance that the learner already has much of the knowledge or skill – the motivated individual can self-coach to some large degree.

CHECKING PROGRESS

Before we move on to considering the range of techniques open to us, and how we can use them, let's pause for a brief Route Review.

ROUTE REVIEW 6

1———10
LOW HIGH

- It will be possible, within my department, for individuals to have a say in the overall training and development plans.

- I can identify the difference between personal and professional development plans, and understand why different timescales may be involved.

- My departmental manager could be interested in helping individuals to develop personal goals, objectives and milestones, where these will add to overall department skills/competencies.

- The Development Support Function is geared up to be able to respond to development need requests from individuals.

- There is the 'mind-set' within our organization which will encourage the use of planning systems as a positive aid.

- Handled correctly, there is the potential within my department for people to mutually help each other more than at present.

- I can think of five ways in which communication could be improved within our organization.

WHAT CAN I DO TO ADVANCE THESE FURTHER?

LEARNING ALONG THE WAY

There you are, standing at the third or fourth milestone with a group of others, looking on down the track. In the distance, you can see the next milestone – with some pretty rough terrain in between. How do you get there as safely and easily as possible?

 ## CPD MILESTONE 61 – REVIEWING THE OPTIONS

Some of the group would stay put and wait for a guide to lead them along the way; others might study the maps and the lay of the land, and then proceed cautiously. One of the party might read a step-by-step guidebook on how to avoid the pitfalls, written by someone experienced in the area, while some might prefer to be given a talk on the possible paths to take and then set off tentatively on their own. And there is invariably one who, like my Celtic forefathers, will shout loudly and rush straight through the mud and bushes, in a mad make-or-break dash!

In short, there are different ways of getting from A to B – and different techniques to apply. No single one is definitely the 'correct' or only way. Some may be less appropriate than others for a given situation – but can probably still be applied. An awareness of the broader range of options certainly helps decision making and problem solving along the way. When things don't work out the way you expected, this more informed awareness makes lateral thinking and problem solving easier.

CPD MILESTONE 62 – THE HYPOTHETICAL DEVELOPMENT CHALLENGE

We have been referring to learners as individuals – and must treat them as such. Imagine that you have lined ten individuals up and said 'Here's £750 each. I want you to go away and, within ten days, return proficient in skill x. You can have a maximum of two days off work. Here is a list of the objectives you must achieve and a specification of the competency level which we expect. You will all have to pass a test set at these competency levels, or you will have to pay us back the £750.'

THE RESPONSE

I would expect perhaps around five or six of the learners to book themselves on one or other course where the specified objectives matched the ones on our sheet as closely as possible. However, I would similarly expect the remainder to choose from a range of alternative techniques. One might buy a book on the subject and learn by self-study and practice; while another might seek out a learning centre and study the subject through open learning. Yet another might hire a distance-learning package and study at home. A slightly more enterprising individual could perhaps arrange for a friend to tutor him privately, with a long weekend in Amsterdam as the reward for both of them (funded by the £750). Do you see the parallels with our pioneering along the track? A variety of possible techniques exists – and different individuals will naturally select to progress in ways which they identify as being most appropriate to their personal needs.

CPD MILESTONE 63 – SELECTING FROM THE RANGE

The concept of triangular integration is built round acceptance of this range of possible responses. The individual will have ideas of how they wish to learn:

- ○ Some find involvement within a group highly motivating.
- ○ Others find that they can pace themselves better when studying alone.
- ○ Some would prefer working along with a mentor, either totally or

periodically during practical reinforcement stages of the overall learning process.

○   Some find technology-based learning a positive benefit, while others might rely on human interactions.

○   Some might even get a buzz from discovering things as they progress – the self-help that we were mentioning earlier.

No one technique is the 'correct' or 'best' way. All are possible for individuals to select as *their* preferred style (even though it may not be yours).

 ## CPD MILESTONE 64 – INTRODUCING OBJECTIVITY INTO THE SELECTION

Some techniques will be more appropriate for some learning areas than for others; for example, it might not be appropriate to use self-study methods to learn highly interactive skills. Similarly, a large-scale seminar in an auditorium may not be the best way to learn skills requiring practical and/or written reinforcement. At this relatively early stage of making a range of options available to learners, we would not necessarily expect them to be widely informed about the options and implications, or able to confidently match subject and content with preferred techniques. This is where the Development Support Function (DSF) comes in.

SUPPORT FROM THE DSF

The perceived role of the DSF is to provide the back-up and support for this selection process. You are the experts, who know the range of techniques which can be applied to given subject areas and can establish how the subject area may be subdivided into modules. You can map potential learning paths through the variety of different modules available on any given subject, and indeed use your professional skills to both select commercial materials and design in-house programmes to create these modules.

Example

When working for a London training consultancy company, we used to run a course on the design of learning materials. Part of this included a review of the 'strengths and weaknesses of the different media techniques'. I now realize the flaw in this title. It is not the medium or technique which has strengths and weaknesses – they are all effective when applied within the parameters of their potential. The skill we must apply is in matching the information, activity or development discussion with the most appropriate single technique or medium – or combination – to give the most effective transfer. We must also be aware that some will find it hard to make the leap to empowerment, having only experienced formalized course provision up to this point.

Consider the following:

○ A step-by-step skill which individuals can learn at different speeds may be best imparted using some form of structured self-study method.

○ Learning which requires a potential change in attitudes must incorporate the facility for the learners to question and discuss reservations throughout the learning process.

○ Practical skills learning must include periodic related exercises to reinforce the steps in the learning, in as realistic a way as possible.

○ Group discussions will help to cement the range of applications of 'soft skills' such as communication, problem solving, team leading and so on.

○ Learning new procedures is assisted by having a combination of steps set out visually for reference and a range of application exercises to practise.

○ Learning which involves discussion and the progressive build-up of information, requires a clear means of displaying this information as it develops.

○ Generally speaking, learning and motivation benefit from variety, which should encourage us to apply a range of options during the overall learning event.

○ Some learning, where there are established options or progressional steps, can benefit from interactive techniques such as multiple choice, interactive video or technology-based training (TBT).

○ Some preliminary factual learning can be achieved using pre-course, self-learn methods, in order to reduce the time actually spent on classroom/practical activities.

CPD MILESTONE 65 – SELECTING HORSES FOR COURSES

A good trainer will match horses from his stable with particular race courses which have prevailing conditions – some horses run better on soft ground, others better on the flat and so on. We too must keep an open mind when matching learner and method – and indeed subject/ skill and method.

When designing and producing learning programmes to satisfy a range of objectives, my greatest successes have involved programmes incorporating a range of modules, with various techniques and degrees of interaction between learner and mentor/tutor.

OFFERING SELECTION OPTIONS, WHERE FEASIBLE

Where possible, a choice of modules (which apply different techniques) allows each learner to select their preferred technique at each stage of learning. More realistically, providing a variety of different techniques within a linear programme at least ensures that no learner gets stuck in a difficult or inappropriate learning style.

The dream of the director of the CBT company I worked for was to be awarded the contract to handle 'all the training for a company like ICI'. The possibilities that some people dislike using CBT as a learning medium, and that some subjects are learned better using human interaction and discussion just didn't enter his equation!

One of the benefits of 'thinking DSF' is that you take this complete range of options into consideration when providing objective solutions across the board. It's big-picture thinking again. At one of the educational technology conferences I attended, I saw someone wearing a button badge with the slogan:

Educational Technology is the answer – now, what is the question?

SELECTION AND THE HIDDEN AGENDA

There are many who, like the director mentioned above, honestly do believe that *all* learning can be achieved using computer-based technology. We will equally be conscious of training companies who pack hundreds of delegates into an auditorium to learn 'seven tips to break negotiating deadlock' and similar claims. Many companies still firmly believe that training courses are the only method of transferring knowledge. This single-mindedness is sometimes more closely linked with company investment in specific facilities and resources, rather than with any objective judgements. We really need to inspire a flash of enlightenment here.

CPD MILESTONE 66 – OVERVIEWING THE 'LEARNING BIG PICTURE'

We're back with our multi-faceted thinking again: I'd like at this point to set out some features of the different techniques which are available, aimed at the prospective learners in our triangle. It might be useful to use as a cross-reference guide to show learners and manager/mentors, who might need some help in understanding the scope available, before being in a position to relate techniques to specific learning needs.

The techniques range may be viewed from a variety of different aspects:

○   Each individual learner may prefer certain techniques over others.
○   Some techniques will be more applicable for some subject/skills areas than others.
○   Some learning techniques will be more appropriate for specific company situations.
○   Combinations of techniques will be seen as appropriate for some development areas.
○   Mentors may feel more confident applying some techniques over others.
○   Overall organization of some techniques will be more feasible than others.

No doubt, there are other viewpoints – it's a case of finding the point of balance between what the individual wants and what the providers can realistically offer, with each striving to be as flexible as possible. Let's review the range available.

CPD MILESTONE 67 – SELF-STUDY

Self-study can have varying degrees of structure. In the light of the other techniques which follow, we will take self-study as being driven largely by the individual learner, with perhaps a set of objectives, a reading list, suggested learning aids, ideas for practical reinforcement and so on, supplied by the DSF and/or the mentor.

Selecting and applying these suggestions, individuals can study at their own pace, using reference materials, making notes and liaising with the mentor/manager in order to gain practical reinforcement on the job as appropriate.

This technique requires a fairly high level of motivation on the part of the learner, with a clear idea of the purpose, objectives and outcomes of the learning area. An accompanying statement, giving pointers regarding stances, beliefs, policies and procedures and other elements to look out for in the chapters indicated, will help the learner read more positively and achieve the required outcomes. Many will find it hard to study in this way – talk to someone who is doing an Open University or distance learning degree course. Within our definitions, these use self-study methodologies applying a fair degree of structure and guidance, best described as 'self-study with overtones of open learning' (see the next CPD Milestone).

CPD MILESTONE 68 – OPEN AND DISTANCE LEARNING

Open and *distance learning* apply a more structured approach than self-study, with detailed programmes which the learner will work through. The programmes usually contain some degree of multiple-choice response and can have branched areas of additional or remedial information to which the learner is directed, depending on the responses given. A note of caution here: I have seen several college-based 'open learning' programmes which are along the lines of 'Read chapter three, respond to the following question and pass your response to your tutor for comment'. I would consider this to be self-study.

Open learning has a more progressive structure. Its design includes statements flowing into examples, followed by question sections linked with confirmation of the answers (with remedial explanations where required). Open learning can use text workbooks or can be more technology based, applying interactive video, audio visual or TBT.

AUGMENTING MATERIALS TO MATCH OBJECTIVES

There is little point in any DSF spending time reinventing the wheel where there are commercial packages available on a certain subject. The development support function must however monitor and evaluate these for suitability against established objectives and criteria, as many packages are fairly generalized; some of the practical examples may be inappropriate for particular businesses or industries, making it difficult for these learners to relate.

Sometimes, a large proportion of a learning package *will* be appropriate – it is thus the task of the DSF to identify the areas of shortfall which are either missing or inappropriate to the learner's need, and compensate for these. This probably will involve the production of supplementary material (perhaps in the form of a simple workbook). On a copyright note, it is perfectly acceptable to do this, as long as you do not interfere with the structure or content of the existing commercial package.

SPOTTING THE DIFFERENCE

What is the difference between open and distance learning? Distance learning is a more detailed form of open learning, and is designed for the learner who will be studying more remotely as an individual. For example, a package for use in a company learning centre, where there is direct administrative and tutor back-up to elaborate as required, could be at the level of general open learning detail.

Think, however, of a package being used on an off-shore oil rig, or in someone's home, with very limited direct support available to answer queries and discuss options. This distance learning package must include a variety of possible options and detailed explanations, in order to be more 'stand alone'. From the design and development point of view, these become more time-consuming to produce, as the designer must identify and elaborate upon the various 'wrong' options, using branching techniques.

THE RANGE OF OPEN LEARNING TECHNIQUES AVAILABLE

Do not feel that open/distance learning materials must be 'high-tech' to be successful; there are some very effective workbooks available, although a well-produced interactive video, applying branching, can allow the learner to select from a range of options.

It's the content, level and applicability of any learning material which is crucial – I've never totally agreed with McLuhan's assertion that 'the medium is the message' and would even go so far as to suggest that on occasion the medium *clouds* the message. For this reason, when reviewing any learning programme, be very clear of your expected objectives and intended outcomes *before* starting to view the material.

 ## CPD MILESTONE 69 – TRAINING COURSES

A training course is composed of a mixture of input, discussion, written and/or spoken exercises and practical involvement. To meet our cognitive learning criteria, it is necessary to have a combination such as this, in order to give us our application stage and other reinforcement stages. By the nature of the subject matter, some courses will be biased towards one or other technique – the overall effectiveness of the course may suffer where this bias has swung too strongly and subjectively towards one extreme.

COURSE AND CONFERENCE – THE DIFFERENCE

One of the possible flaws which feature in current CPD initiatives is a rather bland requirement to complete 'x' days of training annually to update and expand skills. Attendance at conferences also seems to be considered by some to be equal to attendance at a structured, interactive course. I would question this direct comparison: apart from the title, conference organizers are sometimes fairly unaware of the actual content of the various presentations given by the range of 'keynote speakers' on the conference platform, resulting in a rather non-holistic outcome.

Of course, very effective conferences take place – especially those organized by professional bodies, where key speakers are carefully and knowledgeably selected, and objectives and overall subject and content relationships monitored. There are also delegates who definitely prefer this form of learning, as they can select areas and speakers which interest them, gaining insight in a concentrated manner.

EVALUATING THE QUALITY OF A COURSE OR CONFERENCE

How can you judge the quality of a course or conference, prior to the event? One indication is the amount of detail, stated session objectives and general signs of overall planning and intention given in the pre-event documentation. A clear overall structure, with integrated plenary sessions giving conference delegates an opportunity to discuss detail, can also be taken as a measure of its possible effectiveness. Too much emphasis on any associated trade exhibition might indicate a bias towards commercial priorities.

It is likely that a course may have been run before – in which case you can perhaps talk to someone who has attended a previous event. This is probably of more value than reading quotes from evaluation forms (referred to as 'happy sheets' in the trade!), as these can be easily manipulated by the course provider.

LARGE-SCALE SEMINARS

Another form of event – a cross between a course and a conference – is gaining in popularity. This is the *large-scale, one-day seminar*, where some charismatic speaker speeds through a wide range of 'Three tips to . . .'; 'Five ways to . . .'; 'Six strategies for . . .' and so on. From the behaviourist point of view, they are giving you the knowledge, which permits some comprehension. From the objectives achievement point of view, they can certainly be said to be achieving their basic-level objectives, but meaningful interaction is usually lacking, due to large delegate numbers. Linked with this, there is a distinct feeling that a major motivation is in getting the maximum number of delegates through the doors. Work out what they're earning in a day and you'll see what I mean.

These large-scale seminars are a prime example of events which result in the 'halo effect': enthusiasm from delegates at the climax and directly after the event, with this 'high' fading rapidly for a worryingly large percentage of delegates. Many of these in the late 1990s culminated in delegates engaging in 'energy-raising', 'life-enhancing' activities such as fire walking or breaking bricks. Cases of hospitalization brought a glint of reality to these rather stupid end-objectives.

Where CPD recording continues to be biased towards attendance rather than outcome, all these events will tend to be rated equally. The popularity of these seminars may even increase until such time as people start considering continuing professional development more objectively and pragmatically. With the focus shifting towards *applied outcomes*, however, we are gradually moving towards big-picture thinking.

WORKSHOPS

Perhaps the final form of training course which should be considered is the *workshop*. By their nature, they are practically-based, but again the formats and degrees of structure can vary depending to some degree on the subject matter. A practical skill workshop such as cake making, welding or sheep shearing should follow a sequence of demonstration, guided and then solo practice, with remedial input as it implements the various competencies which are planned.

You can also find workshops on more cognitive subject areas, such as counselling, presentation skills and problem solving. They should follow a similar progressional structure – with input sessions as well as discussions, case studies and simulated practical exercises. If there is too high a proportion of freestyle group discussion sessions, you may want to examine the projected objectives and outcomes, to ensure that they meet your needs. Look for evidence of a structure and target outcomes.

 ## CPD MILESTONE 70 – CRITERIA FOR COURSE TYPE AND TECHNIQUE EVALUATION

So, what is the overall moral regarding attendance on the whole range of courses available?

Consider the following:

○ Be selective – establish your own required objectives, priorities and outcomes before reviewing the course objectives on offer.
○ Where appropriate, select events which permit you to apply your learning practically, and receive feedback on these attempts.
○ Consider the maximum number likely to be present at the event and review this against your preferred learning atmosphere and need for interaction.
○ Review the quality of the advertised speaker/tutor – and consider the effects of having only one tutor for a prolonged event (which are better where there is interaction).
○ If you are in doubt, get the DSF to contact the course provider and seek clarification of your questions *from someone who knows*

about the course content. If this is not forthcoming, I suggest that you try elsewhere.

EVALUATING EVENTS

Many courses are available, provided by commercial training providers, colleges, specialist individuals and others. It is difficult to judge their quality – you can ask someone who has attended that particular course but, because the quality of an interactive type of course is dependent on the delegates as well as the tutor, the quality can fluctuate between courses. I have run repeat courses with varying degrees of success, relative to the depth to which the delegates became involved in the practical exercises and discussions – and probably the variability of my dynamism as well.

TIME IS MONEY

Length is important as well – if you can get what you need in one day, including practical reinforcement, don't feel that you need a three-day course. I have been involved with courses run by colleges and parallel commercially-based providers, where one started with the premise that it had to be a two-year, or three-term or five-day course . . . and then end up casting around to find subject areas to fill the time. On a parallel tack, I used to run courses for one of the national utility providers whose employees attending courses considered it their God-given right to have four days' residential training in a hotel every year, with all the trimmings.

INTERNAL COACHING AND MENTORING

Mentoring has been in existence since 'God spake to Adam', but in the personal and professional development context, it's perhaps only become apparent in the last ten to twenty years. Coaching has, of course, been around in the sporting and educational worlds for a long time but again, it is relatively new in business training. How would we define the key difference?

CPD MILESTONE 71 – COACHING

A coach takes the skill which an individual currently has and works with them to develop it further. This involves assisting the individual to evolve and improve current skills and techniques rather than trying to copy *your* way of doing something, which may not be right for the learner. For example, each individual will hold a golf club slightly differently for a comfortable swing – the coach would not force the learner to hold the club exactly as they do. When coaching someone in a foreign language, one would build on the learner's current vocabulary and encourage discussion to expand confidence.

In order to be an effective coach, skills and techniques must be learned; perhaps one of the most important ones is being able to hold back from telling the individual exactly what to do from your own perspective and to concentrate instead on building the individual's existing skills – this certainly requires development and practice. Having said that, I'm sure you can doubtless identify coaches in the sporting world who have probably not had any formal training – but they have in the main had years of experience, both of team working with others and being coached themselves.

 ## CPD MILESTONE 72 – MENTORING

I have already referred to mentoring – indeed the mentor represents one of the corners of our integrated triangle. An informed mentor can transfer knowledge or skills to someone who is not currently at that level of knowledge or skill. This transfer is carried out in an informal, 'hands-on' way, with the learner (sometimes referred to as the 'mentee') being helped to apply the new learning on the job, with direct practical reinforcement being in the course of the learner's daily work.

WHEN DOES A MENTOR BECOME A MENTOR?

There are different schools of thought as to who a mentor should be. Some consider that the mentor should be senior to the learner, with a one-to-one, ongoing learning relationship developing between the two. This relationship is sometimes used to fast-track someone for rapid promotion through an organization.

I maintain that anyone with a body of knowledge or skill can act as a mentor to anyone else who requires that knowledge or skill. Status, age and other similar criteria are not important. Thus, we have the situation where a supervisor is inducting a new employee in the safety procedures for the company. That same day, the newcomer (who happens to be something of a computer expert) could be showing the supervisor how to produce visuals using Powerpoint. The switch of roles is natural, if status is not an issue.

THE 'BUDDY' RELATIONSHIP

The mentor/learner association (sometimes referred to as a 'buddy' relationship) is thus a fairly informal one. It is not necessary to train a mentor in presentation skills and other similar formalized competencies which we might expect a tutor/trainer to possess.

The competent mentor should possess some knowledge of the progressional structure of learning (our cognitive theory again – but in very simple terms), an awareness of the importance of regular reinforcement through practical application and a sympathetic, helpful nature; with these, the ability to mentor should evolve progressively.

One aspect to watch out for is any tendency for the mentor to use little shortcuts, unique techniques and other procedures which don't appear in the operator's manual. There is no question that standards are usually being maintained but mentors sometimes don't realize that these shortcuts can only be applied successfully after a lot of experience. Initial mentoring must 'follow the manual'. Any advanced tips and techniques can come later, once the learner has gained experience.

 ## CPD MILESTONE 73 – THE LIMITLESS SCOPE OF MENTORING

Thinking back to our triangular integration and multi-faceted situation again, the potential for mentoring is immense. In the triangle, we have the mentor being supported by DSF in providing knowledge/ skill transfer to the learner. But, as we have established above, a mentor can also be a learner, and vice versa. Indeed, individuals within the DSF can also be both mentor and learner. It's down to establishing strengths and competencies on the one hand and shortfalls and priority needs on the other. The rest is dependent on a DSF brokering service – and appropriate support. Give it a try.

CPD MILESTONE 74 – ALTERING OUR PERSPECTIVE

Let's review our learning techniques:

- ○ Self-study
- ○ Open learning ⎱ both involving a wide range of AV, text
- ○ Distance learning ⎰ and computer-based techniques
- ○ Training courses (from theoretical seminar to practical workshop)
- ○ Coaching
- ○ Mentoring

There are of course many different specific learning techniques around, such as accelerated learning, NLP (neuro-linguistic programming) mind-mapping and so on, all described in great detail elsewhere. In any event, these tend to be techniques which can be applied within the range of methodologies above – at this stage, we are concerned more with matching methods to individual needs as effectively as possible.

CPD MILESTONE 75 – THE SELECTION PROCESS

As we have established when considering mentoring, the whole concept of mixing and matching development and learner needs is one that requires close consideration in order to get over initial barriers. Many companies view training provision as a matrix completion exercise: a vertical list of departmental personnel down one side of the grid with a horizontal list of available courses along the top. Stars in the boxes indicate necessary courses which have been identified for each particular individual, with a red spot or similar when they have completed it. A similar format and mind-set is applied by managers during appraisal: 'Here are the available courses . . . which will we put you on/do you want to go on?'

There's nothing intrinsically wrong with this approach of course but it is rather limiting. Traditionally, when applied to forms of widescale training and development which must be achieved satisfactorily by large numbers, it is the easiest form of administration. It is, however, not the only way – nor is it necessarily the most efficient or effective. In my view, it can easily become another case of administration driving requirements. The implicit attitude associated with 'analysing needs' in this way is poles apart from placing an individual on identified modules from a complete learning programme, selected to meet specific needs/objectives. This, I believe, is the way forward.

 ## CPD MILESTONE 76 – VIEWING THE BIG PICTURE

Looking down the track from above once more, we can see all those individual paths interweaving as they progress forward. It's a bit like animal tracks in a field. If you look at a field which contains sheep or cattle, you will find beaten trails which they tend to follow. Some walk in a column behind one another along the trail, while others range about, although still moving in the general direction of the majority. Speeds vary and periodically the lead will be taken over by different individual animals.

This is the effect of our development paths. As developing individuals, we are all progressing basically in the same direction, within set parameters but at varying speeds. Sometimes, large numbers are directed along a uniform path for a while, in order to develop general skills. These might include areas such as company induction training, basic computer skills, health and safety, and product knowledge. Cost-effectively, these can be best provided using larger-scale training methods, such as courses or seminars.

We must at the same time acknowledge that this method will not be effective or time-efficient for some of these individual learners, who may require additional assistance or support. Some others may prefer an approach based more on self-learning.

INDIVIDUAL PATHS ALONG THE TRACK

At other times, there will be a loosely-associated group of individuals, heading in the same general direction. When we get to this method of progress, we need to examine individual needs more closely, responding directly to specific shortfalls. It's at this level that we should start thinking of progressing from the matrix approach towards individual development planning, using the CPD planning concepts we have been considering. Through this, we can match shortfall with modular input, individual pace with available processes, and preferred techniques with individual learning styles. We are still considering the needs of each individual – but at a much more specific level.

RAPID RESPONSE

If you visualize the constantly-moving body of individuals in our track in detail, you will doubtless be able to identify the occasional individuals who are standing still, perhaps looking back along their path with a puzzled expression, or, worse still, retracing their steps. These individuals require the rapid response unit of coaching or mentoring to get them moving tentatively forward again. And they need it *now*!

Example

Where the holistic effect is beginning to take hold, you will also notice people talking to and assisting each other as they progress together. This is informal mentoring – at the level of people just helping each other naturally – which appears when co-operative thinking is alive in the department.

When working on a project involved with the introduction of a new computer system within a company, I was an associate member of an internal team of trainers, designing the training programme. There were the usual glitches and plan slippages in the software and as the sacrosanct launch date came ever closer, heightened stress levels were plainly visible.

In this atmosphere of panic and brave faces disguising fear, Frank (a hardware technician) stood as a solid rock. I lost track of the number of times that Frank came to the rescue, producing some visuals here, printing off materials there, getting moody black boxes to behave themselves and generally remaining the sane anchor stone when the storms were raging around him. There was no pressure on Frank to help – indeed, if he had been a 'more than my job's worth' kind of guy, he could have easily refused. However, he enjoyed helping, just for the sake of it. As long as we nurture people like Frank and don't abuse their assistance, we should gradually get more and more like-minded people – perhaps you will join the band yourself!

BIG-PICTURE THINKING

Big-picture thinking helps us consider options objectively and flexibly. It uses a broad reference base, a lateral-thinking approach and a capacity to regularly revisit progress to see whether there is a better way of doing things. It is greatly assisted by the control and elimination of hidden agendas. As with all new and dynamic processes, it progresses best where given universal support. Positive thinking will acknowledge the possibility of mistakes being made along the way –

while at the same time channelling energy towards correcting the errors and progressing once more. This is how we should be expending our energy rather than searching after the event for scapegoats to blame.

TIME OUT

So, are you ready for flexible thinking? Do you have the mind-set to be a fluidly-moving member of the triangle? Do you think that the atmosphere can be developed within your workplace to get this whole thing moving forward? Can your company – or even departments within your company – cope with the concepts?

Make two lists: one setting out the benefits of trying this new approach, and the other identifying the possible blocks. Don't force it – just let the ideas flow. Try to discuss the concepts with a colleague, perhaps someone who has also had the opportunity to read this book. Now, weigh up the benefits as well as the potential blocks and see if you can still see a way forward.

If you can, write down some of your key and immediate priorities.

SELECTING THE PROPER EQUIPMENT

Before we continue further, let's review progress.

ROUTE REVIEW 7

1————10
LOW   HIGH

■ The company where I work is (or could be) using a variety of different learning techniques.

■ The potential is there for individuals to learn by self-study, and open and distance learning, with time off to do so.

■ The DSF training department is capable of arranging a variety of different responses, materials and techniques.

■ I can discuss the appropriate applications of open and distance learning and the various forms of training courses.

■ I can describe the key differences between coaching and mentoring and discuss how I would carry out a mentoring assignment for a selected subject.

■ I can describe a subject area where a combination of different techniques could be applied to the learning programme.

■ I feel that I could encourage others to try to apply these techniques for a particular learning programme.

NOW WE'RE READY TO GET INVOLVED IN THE REAL DETAIL OF MOVING OUR DEVELOPMENT FORWARD.

THE PROPER EQUIPMENT

Having the correct equipment for any particular exercise is very important, as is using the most appropriate techniques. How many of us have struggled with an old pair of pliers to slacken a seized bolt – which would have turned easily using the correct sized wrench and a spot of oil? How many of us have tried vainly to programme the video recorder from memory, where reference to the step-by-step manual would have us up and running in no time at all? How many of us have sat through sections of a two- or three-day training course thinking 'this section's not really relevant to me'?

 ## CPD MILESTONE 77 – GETTING THE CORRECT COMBINATION

In the previous chapter, we briefly considered a range of techniques which can be applied to meet the wide variety of learning situations. Prior to that, we reviewed the different ways that individuals will respond to their own learning needs, as well as those of others. We now want to spend some time marrying the two concepts together – in other words, selecting the most appropriate equipment for any specific expedition.

Without labouring the analogy, think of the difference between the organization required for a fortnight-long expedition abroad ... and for a Sunday trip to the local hills. In some ways, the major trip would involve a lot more organization, resources, applied techniques and expenditure than the Sunday jaunt. However, in some ways, both events would require very similar types of resourcing, such as map reading and planning, selecting general equipment and arranging transport and basic supplies. The same comparisons are relevant where supporting major and individual learning events.

CPD MILESTONE 78 – MATCHING INDIVIDUAL NEEDS WITH TRAINING OBJECTIVES

We considered the value of 'thinking objectively' earlier in the book. Let's bring this to the foreground again by considering an example, which is based on a real assignment which I carried out several years ago. The purpose of the exercise is to consider the steps and stages – if you focus on these, you can easily apply the same process to identify and respond to your own unique problem.

Example

Let's think of a communications/problem-solving exercise. The message on the answering service was deliciously vague: 'We have a communications problem – things need sorting out.' When I returned the call, the person I spoke to couldn't really add much flesh to the bones. Let's visit the client and get to the root of the problem.

QUESTIONS, QUESTIONS

Think of some of the initial questions we might ask:

○   What exactly is the communications problem?
○   Is there a fault with the phones?
○   Do people e-mail each other rather than talking face-to-face?
○   Are there regular team meetings to discuss progress – and are they discussions, or are they simply a monologue from the leader?
○   Is there a proper company communication network to keep people informed of developments as they happen, as opposed to the quarterly newsletter?
○   Can people in positions of authority get the message across clearly?
○   Does head office understand regional priorities?
○   Are the people who should be listening and reacting, *actually* listening and reacting?

In short, can we identify the *real* problems and can we establish the real objectives and competency levels which we aim to achieve?

CPD MILESTONE 79 – PLANNING THE STRATEGY ROUTE

You may have heard of 'communication audits', where we attempt to establish both scientifically and statistically what the real problems are – and what their relative importance is. Some data will be established through interview and questionnaire, so it may not be totally objective; we should be able to filter out some subjectivity, however.

Consider some of the more detailed questions which we might ask:

- Are there regular team/departmental meetings?
- If so, are these effective?
- If not, why not?
- Are you given regular updates when things are changing?
- Are you allowed to rearrange priorities in these circumstances?
- Is such communication two-way, involving active listening?
- Are new policies, procedures and so on set down in writing for reference?
- Is new communication technology being used in a positive way?
- Is the key problem at some individual level or is it a company-generated problem?
- Are you being as specific about the problem as possible?
- Is one person's communication solution creating problems for others?
- Are you aware that people are communicating at the correct level?
- Is there any feedback system to register difficulties at an early stage?
- What would you consider the company's key communication strategy to be?
- Who would the main driving force be, to ensure its success?
- Are there impressive-looking policies and procedures which aren't applied properly?
- How would you suggest they should be applied, for more effective results?
- Are your suggestions realistic and capable of widespread implementation?

The list will expand further, as the actual problem becomes clearer.

APPLYING QUESTIONING TECHNIQUE

Questioning is a case of focusing on the potential problem, listening to the responses and probing laterally in an ever-deepening way to get to the root of the problem. Do not fix on preconceived ideas, or indeed priorities which you might have been told at the outset of the exercise. When one starts discussing a problem with a full range of employees/participants, the actual problem is often quite different from that perceived by the manager. It is often hard to convince the manager that they should reconsider the scenario afresh. Preconceived ideas are sometimes very difficult to change!

 ## CPD MILESTONE 80 – CASE STUDY

Let's focus more sharply on the scenario, which is based on an assignment which I developed with a client. The general scenario was a stores department within a major UK company which was principally involved in a specific form of engineering.

THE BACKGROUND

At the point when I was invited to discuss the problem with the stores manager, the need was simple and apparently obvious: 'The staff don't think or take responsibility for anything – they need training in problem solving. Their communication is poor too.'

As I discussed the situation in greater detail with the manager, he painted a pretty depressing picture: a backlog of incomplete requisitions due to poor ordering, staff not responding to requests, an unacceptable level of absenteeism, complaints from the supervisors that staff would not make decisions about anything and several incidents when staff had been rude to senior members of other departments. A wide range of problems – but only a fraction of them appeared to be involved directly with a need for training in problem solving. There did seem to be some communication issues, however. It was evident that the problem was deeper than initially identified.

THE PLOT THICKENS

When I discussed the situation with a few of the supervisors, I began to see a broader picture. There *was* a problem with staff not taking the initiative, but this was caused largely by the fact that company policy was often decided 'on the hoof' by managers – responding to needs as they happened, with nothing set down in writing.

The company had relatively recently taken delivery of a new internal e-mail system which, as its use became more popular, was achieving slower and slower response times. There were also only two terminals in the stores department, for the use of a total of eight members of staff, including the supervisors.

The computerized procurement system and schedule of parts and other items had been recently upgraded with, unsurprisingly, glitches in the system. There were also contradictions with the old system, which staff were used to using, as well as several key operations which had been omitted in the new system. The plot was thickening.

GETTING TO THE HEART OF THE MATTER

Moving on to discuss matters with several members of staff, I was immediately struck by their concern for getting things sorted out – and the range of suggestions which they provided. They evidently had no problem with problem solving, or decision making. Going back to the supervisors' comments, I began to suspect the technology: first, the e-mail system. The software had evidently been under-designed and couldn't even cope with present volume of use – it would be totally inadequate in the future.

Due to poor training, there was a widespread tendency to use the mass circulation principle, copying the majority of messages to the majority of people. As well as slowing the system down through sheer weight of messages, it was creating the situation where individuals were having to read around forty e-mail messages daily, with only a fraction really relevant. A scarcity of screens in the stores department caused long delays for individuals accessing their messages, and as a result, they often missed the really important ones.

APPROACHING A SOLUTION

So the problem was partially technological, coupled with poor technique. This was not so much due to poor training but more to equipment limitations. There certainly was a training need but it appeared to be one of learning how to create messages more effectively and be more selective in their distribution. Once this had been established, we could then reinforce techniques for responding to them.

 ## CPD MILESTONE 81 – THE ANALYSED SOLUTION

Continuing with the example from CPD Milestone 80, when we stood back from the problem to get the bigger picture, we could see a situation where inadequate technology was hindering rather than helping efficiency and causing mammoth frustration. This was resulting in demotivation, with confusion and incorrect operation procedures causing mistakes to be made. This confusion, coupled with vague operating practices, was hindering staff's ability to reach decisions confidently, which resulted in them trying to second-guess what the manager would do in a given scenario. Poor communication had prevented these situations being addressed.

MEETING NEEDS WITH OBJECTIVES

Improving the technology was outside my remit, although I did submit a short report outlining the key faults. As it was evident that technical upgrades would already be required in the near future, they might be able to improve upon these shortfalls for the future. We now had to establish a range of objectives to meet these needs:

As an event outcome, the learner will be competent to:

1. Apply the specified procedures for sending e-mail messages to personnel identified as being key and major secondary respondents only.
2. Practise techniques of reading e-mail messages quickly and effectively, registering those which require response or further reference.
3. Compare and contrast the old and new systems for stock management and ordering, identifying procedures for applying the new system to achieve the key procurement functions.
4. Practise techniques for achieving the key ordering processes listed separately, in order to improve the satisfaction of order completion deadlines by 70 per cent.
5. Discuss and apply techniques for communicating effectively with internal and external clients, both in identifying procurement

needs more specifically for ordering purposes and in keeping clients informed through regular progress reports.

6. Discuss and apply techniques for project management of the ordering process, in order to give prior warning of potential delays and identify potential solutions to circumvent related supply problems.

There are probably others but let's take these as the key objectives. From the training point of view, we can do something concrete to respond to each of these. However, for the outcomes to be successful, there are several prerequisites which must be satisfied. These involve the technology and the establishment of procedures and guidelines for decision making. If these are not resolved first, the problems remain primarily those of ineffective systems, incomplete procedures and inconclusive management decision making – which no amount of staff training could improve directly.

CPD MILESTONE 82 – APPLYING MORE DETAILED ANALYSIS

Having established the objectives, we would then proceed to identifying the most appropriate learning techniques for each. Let's review each objective briefly in turn. The reference numbers relate to the numbered objectives above – refer to each in turn before reading the detail below:

1. This is a combination of learning a step-by-step process and considering techniques of identifying key and secondary respondents. The step process can be set out for self-learning in text form – or could be built into the computer system.

   Using either method, it is necessary to have practical reinforcement to give direct practice in using the computer. The identification of key and secondary respondents is probably achieved best as a discussion session, led by the manager as tutor/coach, to establish circulation criteria.

   Once established, the actual procedures for activating this in the computer system can be learned as above, as a step-by-step process.

2. This will be best achieved applying an initial theoretical input to establish criteria and discuss strategies, followed by a practical exercise to reinforce technique. As the theory session will almost

certainly involve discussion, it is probably best achieved as a tutor/mentor-led meeting session. This can then be reinforced practically, using a stand-alone learning module.

3. This comparison of old and new systems, complete with required outcomes and differences in technique to achieve these, will be best presented as parallel step-by-step text guides.

    These can be designed on the basis of the learner having had experience of the old system (increasing the level of assumed knowledge), with the emphasis therefore on the different techniques required for the new system. After several theoretical exercises, the learner will be given related practical exercises to be carried out on the new system, to reinforce operational procedures.

4. As the actual operational procedures have already been established and practised in (3) above, the emphasis in this module will be on identifying and overcoming potential blocks in completing the ordering process and satisfying deadlines.

    This may be best achieved by running a discussion session where actual examples of delayed order completion are discussed positively in order to identify possible strategies for improving resolution.

    If this session is run by the manager as tutor/coach, it may subtly give the opportunity to cement some of the policies and discuss procedures through to an agreed conclusion, with improved liaison and motivation as a direct spin-off.

5. This is a straightforward communication module. As it is designed specifically round direct procurement activities, it will therefore need to be specially designed and not 'off-the-shelf'.

    As a key issue will be establishing the accuracy of detail necessary to avoid errors on the computer system, thus maintaining progress, an awareness of the system operational processes (reference 3 and 4 above) is necessary before proceeding with this module.

    Applied communication technique can be further reinforced using role-play exercises set within a procurement context.

6. This module will present basic project management and problem-solving processes – and will again rely on prerequisite knowledge of the ordering process. Although the processes can be presented as theory input (as a self-study 'mini-module' to be completed prior to a workshop session, for example), it can also be achieved

using normal tutoring techniques. However this factual input is achieved, the second, workshop stage must involve relevant case-study examples to practise the application of the theory – and discuss alternative strategies where relevant.

 ## CPD MILESTONE 83 – REACHING REAL CONCLUSIONS

Through our auditing process – which amounts to basically just speaking to a variety of people rather than one, asking structured questions, keeping an open mind and observing the situation broadly and laterally – we have identified the department's need in detail and come up with a list of probable routes and techniques to apply.

PLANNING FOR CONTINUING DEVELOPMENT

In development terms, by identifying the needs in detail first, we have been able to establish the objectives as they should be composed – objectively and in detail – and respond to each with regard to preferred techniques.

Some of these responses may already be available for use – others will undoubtedly have to be designed and produced – but the final learning programme will be appropriate for the needs as identified, and flexible enough to change if required. This, you will see, is a response which is much more specific and detailed than anything we could have produced as a result of the manager's initial statement. It is also meeting the department's specific needs much more precisely than anything which could have been 'taken off the shelf' using the matrix model of preconceived courses.

DETAILED ANALYSIS RESULTS IN SPECIFIC RESPONSE

As an external consultant could I please underline this problem of access, which I have experienced in varying degrees on many occasions? This is a plea directed at training departments; that you consider the value in taking a broader view of any potential need prior to identifying the solution, and keeping an open mind about methods of response. This is the essence of 'support function' thinking.

Because training consultants are usually invited in by the training/ DSF department, they tend to liaise directly with this department –

and often with only one individual in the department. I sometimes find it difficult to get additional access to line managers and personnel to check the broader picture. This restricted access could be due to economic limitations, professional pride or internal politics, but the end result is often poorer because of this constraint on viewing the broader picture at the design stage. Talking to a range of personnel will invariably improve the development needs analysis – and response.

BUILDING UP YOUR RESOURCE BANK

If you consider the bigger picture objectively, you will be better prepared to respond to learning/development needs as specifically and effectively as possible. Having prepared these modular responses, you can reuse them to meet similar needs in the future, while at the same time keeping an eye on differing priorities which might then require additional or revised modules. There is always a danger that, having 'packaged' some training solution, it then becomes the complete off-the-shelf response to any need bearing that general title – and then you're back to matrix thinking again.

 ## CPS MILESTONE 84 – IMPROVISATION IN THE FIELD

However good your planning or however many contingencies you have allowed for, there is always going to be something cropping up which catches you unawares. This is where improvisation becomes important: it may be that piece of string in the back pocket and your scouting knowledge of knots; it may be that idea for practical involvement to overcome post-lunch torpor; it may be the review of objectives against the needs of a particular group of learners. I've hit problems with this last one.

Example

As a senior consultant with a London-based training course provider in the early 1980s, I was responsible for running a wide range of courses for training officers; each course had a set of objectives, a programme and exercises. It had a distinct structure. In those days, we had quite a range of delegates coming through the system.

Sometimes, we had a preponderance of former line managers or recent graduates, with little direct training experience to date while, on parallel courses, we might have the majority having many years of training experience but who (in those days) had never got round to formal qualifications themselves. I found that, with these latter groups, one could extend the practical exercises and discussion sessions dramatically, taking full advantage of the delegates' experience. This often involved working through solutions to their real problems, which made these groups very interesting and dynamic to work with, as one was in effect incorporating quick-witted, 'thinking-on-one's-feet' consultancy within the structured programme. The application sessions could thus push forward into the higher cognitive levels (analysis, synthesis and evaluation), making the outcome more valuable.

This form of improvisation is, in my opinion, very valuable in the world of training – it stretches everyone to the limit and beyond, although it may create the situation where delegates will only benefit later, once they have had the opportunity to implement and evaluate the applications back at the workplace, in the months after the actual course.

A decade later, I returned as an associate to tutor specific courses for this same consultancy, which had in the meantime gone down the route focusing on gaining national and international standardized qualifications. I entered the world of manual-driven delivery, appraisal forms and desk-based assessments, where everything was prescribed to the last detail and any detours from the manual structure were almost punishable by death! The overall atmosphere had become more assertive and was lacking in that secret ingredient which used to be called *fun*. Of course, whenever my old habits and the presence of some experienced delegates encouraged me to digress to apply these deeper analytical approaches to the exercises, I got into trouble because someone felt it was inappropriate and wasn't on the programme.

 ## CPD MILESTONE 85 – RESPONDING FLEXIBLY TO DIFFERING NEEDS

This flexible approach was yet another incidence of 'horses for courses'. Using a very prescriptive approach is best for learners who have to be led step-by-step along the learning path and who need closely structured reinforcement exercises within the learning process to compensate for lack of experience. Where the experience base is present in the body of learners, however, some elements of any prestructured course will become less important than others and greater value can be achieved discussing situations which they have experienced directly. Within this context, suggested solutions and strategies can be assessed more realistically. Flexibility here is a distinct benefit – I suppose the moral is that the selection and grouping of similar-level delegates is very important.

By all means, do try to stretch the learners' abilities during a formal training course, even to the point of it being slightly uncomfortable at the time. Remember, this will probably be the only time they will have the luxury of spending an extended period of time together studying a particular subject. However, they will have the rest of their lives to implement the concepts learned, so you should be exposing them to as wide a range of knowledge and concepts as possible during the learning experience. The consolidation can come later – with mentoring help as appropriate.

THE PENDULUM CENTRES ITSELF

So, if you have the confidence, improvise. I believe that training is reaching the extremes of monitoring, documentation and bureaucracy and will, as has happened with education, stabilize at an equilibrium point where effective individual outcomes will be considered to be more valuable than an overemphasis on monitored standardization.

The statistical manipulation of standards for political gain may also result in a loss of credibility for those same standards and qualifications. For example, the school inspectorate OFSTED currently expects annual improvements in standard tested results (referred to as SATS). Poor performance by one or two 'educationally challenged' pupils in one school year group can create reduced overall results, comparatively, year-on-year, which is a nonsense.

MEETING THE NEEDS IN THE BROADEST WAY POSSIBLE

Consider the following:

- ○ We must analyse broadly to identify the real development needs.
- ○ We must keep an open mind during this analysis process.
- ○ Setting down objectives will help us plan the development progressively.
- ○ We must be aware of the range of techniques available – and apply them.

- ○ A planned structure coupled with a range of experience allows flexibility.
- ○ A modular response allows both a range of applications and future adaptation.
- ○ Reinforcement using real examples and experience gives improved results.
- ○ We must arrange for ongoing reinforcement and development in the workplace.
- ○ We must maintain our control over the learning structure, priorities and outcomes.
- ○ A flexible, co-operative outlook will allow the best use to be made of resources.
- ○ Say that 'our most important resource is our people' – and really mean it.
- ○ Resist bureaucracy which overshadows the effectiveness of the outcome.

CHARTING PROGRESS

In Britain, a large proportion of outdoor pursuits such as hillwalking and mountain climbing are carried out in a small number of restricted geographic areas. Walkers 'do' the Ridgeway or the Pennine Way. Similarly, climbers 'do' Munros, those mountain peaks which have been charted at over 3000 feet above sea level. Meanwhile, there are miles and miles of little-known or used tracks and paths around the country, where you will only meet occasional like-minded souls as you commune with less popularized Nature.

 ## CPD MILESTONE 86 – THE OVERLYING PURPOSE OF PROGRESS

Is walking some distance over the empty moorlands of Scotland any less of an achievement than covering a measured distance along various recognized and densely-populated routes (such as the Pennine Way) which we read about in the guide books? Not really, although the claim of achievement of the latter may sound more impressive, to those who study such things.

Similar claims and comparisons can and will be made with continuing professional development records, which are applied for very similar reasons, as a register of involvement and achievement along the CPD path we have chosen. Many follow similar learning paths – we are now aware of the breadth of opportunities open to us. Using some form of personalized planners, we can integrate the final recording of progress with the initial strategy plans. This saves duplication of effort – as well as paper.

THE RANGE OF CPD ACTIVITIES

CPD activities cover virtually anything which can be seen to expand one's knowledge, responsibility, decision-making powers and/or competencies. Where we are focusing on outcomes rather than activities, we require a CPD recording system which is sophisticated enough to register these different levels of importance. It is undoubtedly easier to merely record the activity, for example, 'attended such-and-such two-day course', but identifying outcomes will certainly be more valuable, in terms of charted development.

What activities would we consider to be appropriate?

Consider the following:

○   Any position of responsibility, relating to personal or professional activities.
○   Any type of course or conference.
○   Any form of self-study, from guided reading to distance learning.
○   Any additional form of structured learning of any applicable subject matter.
○   Official roles such as becoming a school board member.
○   Direct involvement in the development of others (coaching, mentoring and so on).
○   Involvement in the design and writing of materials structured to inform others.
○   Formal or informal cross-learning of skills parallel to those normally carried out.
○   Direct involvement in the organization of events and activities.
○   Active membership of professional associations, at national and local levels.
○   A developed interest in any transferable hobby or activity.
○   Organized involvement in the general improvement of well-being in others.
○   Evidence of the application of a more holistic/altruistic/co-operative way of life.

COMBINING PERSONAL AND PROFESSIONAL ACTIVITIES

Some of these activities are uniquely personal or professional, while others combine both. I would consider it to be an added benefit where personal and professional development do interact. An example of this might be where an individual extends their mentoring role to giving regular assistance and help on-the-job, 'lending a helping hand' as necessary in order to ensure that learning reinforcement remains as positive and developmental as possible – where co-operative attitudes are developing naturally.

CPD MILESTONE 87 – WHY SHOULD WE RECORD CPD ACHIEVEMENTS?

There are several reasons for recording CPD achievements, some more positive than others. There is, of course, the basic reason of allowing others to monitor your progress. Remember, we are focusing at the level of *outcome* rather than *activity*. I can think of many people who are 'members of such and such a committee', but who rarely say a word or play any active role in the committee's formative activities. People may even engage in these roles quite cynically because they 'look good on the CV' (which is a form of CPD record in its own right). Real accomplishment or outcomes is what job-interview questions, such as 'give an example of where you took the initiative as a committee member', are trying to probe.

Establishing an individual's competency is much the same as the process of mechanically testing a car for roadworthiness. How do many British garages organize this MOT test? They run the full range of checks on the car initially, in order to identify any areas where the vehicle fails. The garage then rectifies these specific faults and, hey presto, the car is qualified to be on the road again. This may not be official policy – but it achieves the required outcome.

CPD MILESTONE 88 – DEVELOPMENT TESTING FOR HUMANS

In development training, we can apply the modular approach which I have been advocating in the same way. First, you carry out competency testing to establish specific shortfalls, then apply modules of remedial or new training as required by that individual, to develop them towards achieving the competency levels. Establishing these competency-level tests is initially hard work but, once created, they can be used uniformly within the organization – or through standardized tests, nationally.

We evidently need some means of recording specific competencies achieved, in order to plan the required input and record its achievement. This is our combined individual development plan and competency achievement record. A CPD system including this amount of detail and allowing this degree of overview of development plan progression, provides a document which all the integrated triangle participants can apply effectively.

 ## CPD MILESTONE 89 – APPLYING A CPD PLANNING SYSTEM

Where we are recording at this level of detail, with the outcomes a natural spin-off from the planning process, the purpose of recording immediately becomes more positive. If you cast your mind back to Part V, you made some notes about the headings which you would select for your personalized planner. Have a look at these again, or if you can't locate them, look at the suggestions which I made in CPD Milestone 56 (p. 69).

These suggested headings, involving objectives, specific responses, key priorities and milestones, indicate the detail which we will add, once the associated outcomes have been achieved. Using this process, the planning stage flows seamlessly forward into the implementation stage, ending with the recording of specific outcomes. This may indicate achievement of that particular competency, or may identify related objectives for further development – in which case the process continues.

MAKING THE ACTIVITY 'VALUE ADDED'

I feel strongly that, to be positive and long-term, any recording and monitoring process must be seen by each participant to add value to their individual development. Where record keeping is being done primarily as an exercise to satisfy others, it becomes a rampant chore. Create too many controls and the individual will channel efforts into attempting to evade them. On the other hand, provide a flexible system which empowers the individual to plan and progress their own development path and you have the motivation necessary to keep the whole thing moving along positively.

CPD MILESTONE 90 – PLANS, REALITY AND LATERAL THINKING

So much for charting our progress at the level of specific activities. What about the overall progress of our development path along that long straight track? Many individuals will progress along the same, or very similar paths: the established learning programmes which are necessary for the uniform and efficient running of an organization.

At times, individual paths will break off from this well-trodden way, to learn individual or advanced skills in order to develop competency levels further. Here, we are entering the higher levels of motivation, with self-actualization encouraging exploration along little-used but identifiable paths. Others might detour from the path to enter a remedial loop, to revisit a particular area which is perhaps proving to be difficult to implement.

CPD MILESTONE 91 – PROBLEM SOLVING TO MAINTAIN PROGRESS

As we have established earlier, being aware of your options makes problem solving – and indeed lateral thinking – much easier. For example, you have progressed to a point along your learning path and the next stage in your programme involves viewing a training video. The video is available but the only video playback unit has developed a fault. Consider some of the options yourself. Must I view it now, before progressing further? Where else could I locate a playback unit? Is there a parallel text learning module I could use? Can I get the necessary information by talking to someone?

The options are there, if you think about it, rather than sitting staring at the faulty equipment, willing it to play! When implementing planned learning, a combination of self-empowerment, an open mind, alternative resource availability and lateral thinking will keep you moving forward along your particular path.

CPD MILESTONE 92 – TRIANGULAR INTEGRATION: IS IT WORKING?

As we've been focusing for some time on the individual response, perhaps it's time while we are charting progress to see whether our triangular integration ideas are still progressing positively.

ROUTE REVIEW 8

```
1————10
LOW   HIGH
```

- Individuals are taking a more active part in their own skills and knowledge development.

- Requests are coming through for specific learning modules to respond to closely analysed individual needs.

- Managers are supporting these individual requests.

- The DSF is managing to respond actively to identified needs – and is working proactively on others to build up a resource bank of appropriate materials and programmes.

- Where individual needs are under discussion, there is active and equal liaison among the three parties.

- The individual's CPD planning and recording system is being used positively and actively by all three parties.

- The CPD system is used as a direct reference point in the run-up to, and during, appraisal sessions.

- Individual requests for support through mentoring and practical involvement are being addressed positively.

- Individuals are making development suggestions proactively, rather than resorting to established solutions.

- Managers are positively supporting the overall concept of providing individual responses to development needs.

AM I NOW GETTING RESPONSE SCORES OF 5 AND 6 OR MORE? IF NOT, WHAT CAN I DO TO MOVE THE SITUATION FORWARD?

CPD MILESTONE 93 – USING THE CPD SYSTEM CONSTRUCTIVELY

Individual CPD plans and records, properly maintained and updated, will be available for reference to both the manager/mentor and the DSF. Using this, the empowered individual will certainly be able to keep driving things forward, requesting assistance, resources and so on, but must remain realistic.

You know how we feel, if we are at our desk and concentrating deeply on some problem, report or whatever, when someone comes up and launches into talking about some pet subject or query. It usually takes us some time to get our head round to thinking about what they are saying – and by then, we've lost the key issues raised in the opening sentences. Bad communication – unreal expectations.

WORKING REALISTICALLY

In the same way, although individuals may be totally wrapped up both in their own development plan requirements and their drive to maintain ongoing progress, they must accept that they are each only one amongst many that the manager and DSF will have responsibility towards. They must not expect an instant response to every request, or that the mentor or DSF staff member is immediately aware of their current CPD detail.

CPD MILESTONE 94 – MEMO/DISCUSSION/ACTION

If individual learners have provided a good set of up-to-date plans and outcome records, to which the mentor or DSF staff member can refer, this will make planning and monitoring easier. I believe in the value of the written word – the three-step *memo/discussion/action* format allows effective progress in any form of communication.

○   *Memo* – Note down the key points, questions, requirements and/ or statements which you want to discuss and send this note to the other party or parties prior to any meeting. At best, they will have read it and have considered the implications and potential outcomes prior to your discussion; at worst, it is a structured reference document for the meeting.

○ *Discussion* – Using the memo as a checklist, you can progress the discussion positively, ensuring some degree of outcome for each issue.

○ *Action* – Register in writing the outcomes and actions which were agreed during the discussion, either noting them on the memo sheet against each item, or as a brief action report/minute. This stands as a statement of future commitment, giving you a concrete reference point (hopefully avoiding any subsequent 'but I thought you said . . .' arguments).

APPLYING THE FORMAT TO CPDS

You'll see that the individual development plan is the *memo* stage of the exercise, setting out the plans and requirements. The *discussion* stage encompasses every level of related conversation, from chance exchanges in the corridor to full-blown appraisal sessions. Finally, the *action* stage is the updated plan document, recording completed milestones and indicating future activities. Overall, we have the individual CPD system working as a living record, accessible to all within the integrated triangle.

 ## CPD MILESTONE 95 – GETTING OUT OF THE MUD

What do you do when you're stuck in the mud? You call for help. What type of help do you need? That depends on the mud and how deeply you've sunk into it! If you're in a normal family car, a trusty Land Rover will usually be sufficient. A lorry, on the other hand, might require a 20-ton 'wrecker truck' to shift it.

SEEKING THE APPROPRIATE HELP

When the learner's development progress gets stuck in the mud, our response should equally be selected to relate directly to the severity of the blockage. Crying 'Wolf' every time, as we know from the story, progressively creates the situation where you are no longer taken seriously when you really do have a problem. When the overall development system is in place, when individual development plans have been mapped out, and when the triangular integration is functioning effectively – then we can select the most appropriate method of getting the individual progressing once more.

TIME OUT

Consider these 'blockage' situations, then try to identify and make a note of appropriate responses:

O   Pressure of work allowing little flexible time during the working day.
O   Lack of equipment/technology to present the learning materials.
O   Lack of understanding of areas of detail after some learning event.
O   Requirement for learning a totally new subject area.
O   Problems with understanding instruction from a particular tutor/mentor.
O   Cost of public training courses.
O   Need for instruction in some very specialized subject area applied in-company.
O   Requirement for ongoing practical on-the-job reinforcement.
O   Individuals requiring greater assistance in monitoring their progress.

THE RANGE OF SOLUTIONS

Some solutions will require attendance on commercially available courses; others will be met by more informal mentoring and coaching. Some will require planned reinforcement exercises; others can be resolved using day-to-day examples as illustration/consolidation. Professional trainer, formal coach, informal mentor, co-operative colleague? Self-assessment, CPD-documented evidence, annual appraisal? Each involves a choice to be analysed and made. What we are striving to identify is the most appropriate response for the particular degree of problem or blockage.

> *Problems are there to test us –*
> *we have the ability, we are conscious of the answer.*
> *If only we have the confidence to proceed.*

■ CPD MILESTONE 96 – USING A CPD SYSTEM POSITIVELY

As we freely acknowledge, recording information for its own sake is a dreadful chore. Increasingly, as has happened recently with income tax, the onus is being placed on the individual to carry out the work, with ever-higher penalties if we don't provide the documentation on time!

JUSTIFYING THE EFFORT

Somehow, expending effort on planning one's future activities and objectives seems a much more positive activity. As the various headings in our CPD formats indicate, applying modules which progress logically and sequentially will permit us to record that progress. It permits all parties in our triangle to check progress against schedules, as well as identifying blocks when they are still minor – and capable of easier resolution.

This is another case of applying 'defensive driving' techniques to planning: we remind ourselves to look and plan ahead. When this forward planning facilitates the most effective response to each individual need, overall motivation remains high.

INTEGRATING PERSONAL WITH PROFESSIONAL

Initially separating personal and professional development issues allows more specific responses to each. Once we have worked on their individual progress, it will often be easier to then amalgamate them consciously for particular activities. We can focus, for example, on leading a more selfless life, helping others where appropriate. We can equally focus on improving our business skills in, for example, customer care. Combining both, we can progress beyond the rather 'automatic' steps and stages (for example, are you fed up of being asked automatically 'is everything all right?' at regular intervals when dining in a restaurant?) to developing a meaningful conversation with the customer, in order to establish their real needs.

Recently, my wife and I were in an electrical superstore walking around different sections looking at a range of items. We were approached three times by the same assistant who used the same opening statement each time, with absolutely no indication that she recognized us from speaking to us two minutes previously! On the other hand, I can think of many service staff who relate and speak to me directly, without resorting to the set 'have a nice day/can I help you' – type phrases.

 ## CPD MILESTONE 97 – OUR CURRENT POSITION ON THE DEVELOPMENT TRACK

As discussed already, we are all at some point on the journey from *belonging* through *assertion* towards *co-operation*. Some of us have moved further along than others, but this is to be expected and accepted. Some may remain in *belonging* mode, others might settle at some level of *assertion*, while others will feel most comfortable when acting *co-operatively*. No one is right or wrong – each represents a balance point in a developing state of mind, a stage in personal development.

Because the human being is a complicated entity, we may find that we function within a range of these dimensions. We may, for example, like a fairly co-operative domestic life, compromising with the wishes of our partner, helping our neighbour or carrying out voluntary work willingly. When at work, however, we may feel that we must act assertively because 'this is what is expected in business'. An effective CPD planning system will help us amalgamate the two.

THE IMPORTANCE FOR PLANNING

Clear maps and plans are helpful for everyone involved in keeping the journey flowing smoothly, with everybody achieving to the best of their ability. Detailed reports help us identify potential blocks and shortfalls which require some form of remedial assistance. They also highlight resources which will be required in the future. In the realms of logistics planning, all this data is used to establish staffing and resource requirements, which can itself be a time-consuming exercise.

In CPD recording terms, the manifestation of this will be the individual development plan, and the progress record. These are valuable and supportive documents, if used well.

Although we have been having regular Route Reviews, it's some time since we've had a Health Check. Let's have one now, before progressing further to consider techniques for reviewing progress.

HEALTH CHECK 3

✓   I can describe and discuss what my key development requirements are.

✓   I know how to produce some form of individual development plan.

✓   I have had initial discussions about my CPD with both my manager/mentor and the development support function (DSF)/training department.

✓   I am clear of the range of learning opportunities open to me – and my preferences.

✓   I understand the benefits of thinking holistically, where combining elements will give a greater end result than that received by completing the elements separately.

✓   I feel empowered to drive my own development plan forward and am confident that I will receive support in achieving this.

✓   I am clear of the analogy of individual paths progressing within the confines of the established way forward – and how my path integrates with those of others.

✓   I can differentiate between the various techniques which are available and can identify ones which will be most appropriate to meet my individual learning needs.

✓   By thinking objectively, I can assess the degree of difficulty and complexity of my different learning needs – and can select appropriate modular responses to suit.

✓   I have taken steps to produce my individual development plan and record and am clear how this will be used as my overall CPD record system.

IS THERE ANYTHING I STILL NEED TO DO TO MAKE SOME OF THESE HAPPEN?

REVIEWING PROGRESS

We have been considering progression along the long straight career track, selecting personal paths as we go, advancing purposefully and opting for appropriate responses to maintain this progress. We have considered at some length the potential benefits of direct liaison between the integrated triangle corners and the need for particular solutions to meet specific needs. However, you may not yet have had an opportunity to actually practise these concepts very much within your work or life situation. As a result, you may not feel in a strong position to review progress.

THE VIEW FROM THE HILL

From this point on, we'll change our position slightly. Let's move to a higher vantage point, to the side of our long straight track, in order to look down upon it and review activities. At Avebury in the southern English county of Wiltshire, lies Silbury Hill, a huge human-made mound which was probably both energy centre and superior vantage point for the activities of the people who lived near Avebury and Stonehenge thousands of years ago. Imagine we are now standing on our vantage point, looking down on the development track and considering the aspirations, goals and the many individual progressional paths which we can see.

 ## CPD MILESTONE 98 – REVIEWING PROGRESS

How can we best review our progress? We need a set of criteria or standards – the milestones which we have already been considering –

which give us measures of time, objectives and competencies (and the degree of their achievement). This will give a comparison of real against expected outcomes. But take note: we are reviewing *outcomes*, thus we cannot accurately measure progress through basic action statements such as 'attending a training course' – it's the outcomes or standards of achievement which are important.

THE COMPLEXITY OF MONITORING INDIVIDUAL PROGRESS

Remember also that these achievements are individual ones. If, instead of our hypothetical Silbury Hill, we were on Mount Olympus viewing the 100-metres running track and all the athletes were starting at the same time, running the same race and crossing the same finishing line, monitoring progress would be relatively easy.

However, individual paths of progress along our track are taking different routes, detours and pauses for consolidation, starting at different times and even occasionally retracing steps quite validly to clarify issues. This makes it absolutely imperative that each individual maintains a detailed CPD system, logging progress towards satisfactory completion. The more specific, the easier it is to identify milestones when achieved.

CPD MILESTONE 99 – RELATING PERSONAL AND PROFESSIONAL DEVELOPMENT

A detailed CPD system will include the greatest amount of subdivision possible between personal and professional development. The two can then integrate closely, as individuals progress towards working co-operatively, with many work-elements combining seamlessly.

Some major companies have gone through phases of recognizing the benefits of open-ended self or personal development in relation to motivation at work, through funding employee involvement in anything from horse riding to skiing or embroidery. Sadly, these have tended to be short-lived, with any temporary motivational benefits killed off by the almost inevitable return to shareholder-driven 're-engineering' and cost-cutting.

THE HOLISTIC INTEGRATION OF PERSONAL AND PROFESSIONAL

Although I would do nothing to discourage these blips of altruism, I would hope that in time the real relationship between personal and professional will be seen to have mutual long-term benefit for both individual and work environment, if allowed to progress.

Currently, business is going through the cycle of equating change with benefit and takeover or amalgamation with increased efficiency, although it has been demonstrated that public opinion can still over-turn business (and political) myopia. I hope that this same public concern will highlight some of the hidden agendas which are impeding holistic progress, encouraging the stability necessary for longer-term development to succeed.

CPD MILESTONE 100 – THE HUNDRED MONKEYS

In the world of self-development, there is a concept called 'the hundred monkeys' principle. This states that initially, if one monkey acts or thinks differently from the pack, he is screeched into submission (as with the 'tall poppy' effect I mentioned earlier). If however, that monkey perseveres and additional monkeys progressively join in, a 'critical mass' number – the hundredth monkey – can tip the balance and change the norm.

Never forget the principle of the hundred monkeys if you feel strongly about something. A confident small voice – yours – can start the flow of change – the story of the Emperor's new clothes is another example of the same principle.

THE VALUE OF LONG-TERM STABILITY

The importance of stability, of creating the atmosphere where matters can evolve naturally and of allowing the holistic effect to progress without threat from hidden agendas seems fairly understandable – it's the way an efficient household or team is run, where everyone is aware of the established ground-rules and any subsequent progress or change is based on these guaranteed benchmarks.

This is what our long straight development track is all about: a known environment within which we can confidently exist, expand and progress. We would not want someone to come along and start throwing up additional barriers, traffic-calming schemes and forests of restriction notices to 'increase our rate of progress along a series of predetermined paths'. However, too prescriptive an approach to competencies, resulting from too formalized ISOs and other forms of national and international standardized qualifications, could tip the balance that way, if we're not careful.

CPD MILESTONE 101 – SPOTTING THE SIGNS OF CO-OPERATION

How do we begin to spot the signs of co-ordination between personal and professional development?

Consider the following:

○ People listen as well as speak during communication, making it two-way and try to respond positively to what they hear.
○ Managers appreciate that staff members can only achieve a finite amount of work in a given time and, through better planning or by prioritizing work requests, allow their staff members to achieve previously agreed goals and projects.
○ Individuals take responsibility for their own work-continuity, analysing and responding to particular needs and problems in order to maintain progress.
○ An individual overrides the personal ego to help someone – or refrains from taking the credit where it can be shared over team involvement in a project.
○ The overall point and effectiveness of the current 'long hours' work ethic is questioned, as to how much additional outcome it produces overall and what its effects are on personal and domestic life long-term.
○ People consciously and actively become involved in mentoring strategies – and are allowed the time to develop them effectively.
○ Individuals are encouraged by their employers to take on part-time roles of responsibility within society, to both expand them as individuals and promote better company/locality relationships.

TIME OUT

Think about each of the points above. Where they involve the individual applying personal development mores within their business life, you should note that these generally extend beyond the development of a new learned skill.

With 'personal development' here, we are thinking at the self-improvement level of living and working co-operatively, helping others, living a more selfless existence, being open and honest and generally living and working to a set of principles. Does that all sound too idealistic? I don't think so. I'm looking for my other ninety-nine monkeys!

CPD MILESTONE 102 – REVIEWING STRENGTHS AND SHORTFALLS

Many years ago, I was running a training course on the design of presentations for advanced audio-visual applications in Dublin and was waxing eloquent about the benefits of objectives. Suddenly, one of the delegates piped up with:

If you aim at nothing, you're sure to hit it.

Yes, I had to think about it for a while as well! He was, of course, right in some ways, although, taken at the extreme, it means that absolutely anything can be justified. A lot of presentations, advertisements and statements in meetings are based upon that premise. Immediately after hearing the information, you think it sounds and/or looks very impressive. It's only later, when you try to respond to it or act upon it, that you realize the lack of content, detail or objective. Can you think of any TV advertisements where you remember the images but can't name the actual product featured? Some car advertisements, perhaps?

CPD MILESTONE 103 – ESTABLISHING A REVIEW SYSTEM

In earlier chapters, we looked at objectives and how they could be used specifically. We also considered the application of milestoning to establish the steps and stages of learning – and applied the different levels of cognitive development. We have considered potential formats to apply these various principles, to create an individual development planner and reviewed how it can then record progress and outcomes.

We have, in short, established a complete process for meeting learning and development needs; establishing strengths and shortfalls and directing progress towards the achievement of specific objectives which are prioritized and graded in order to develop the individual both personally and professionally.

 ## CPD MILESTONE 104 – USING OBJECTIVES TO REVIEW PROGRESS

You may recall that, when we were considering objectives in the early chapters, we underlined the need to be as specific as possible, to identify standards against which to monitor progress and achievement, and to apply the cognitive levels logically.

CASE STUDY: APPLYING OBJECTIVES TO DELIVER AND EVALUATE TRAINING

After joining an American airline catering company as international training manager, I was soon involved in a major project producing a complete training programme for kitchen hygiene and sanitation regulations, which consisted of a manual and several associated audio-visual programmes, published in several languages.

The programme included sections with headings such as 'Personal Hygiene', 'Food Poisoning and the Pathogens', 'Food Handling and Temperature Control', 'Refrigeration of Foodstuffs', 'Cleaning and Sanitation' and 'Food Hygiene Laws and Regulations'.

As an illustrative example, I'd like to take one module of this programme, 'Food Handling and Temperature Control', in order to demonstrate how the objectives and content were developed, and applied to review and evaluate learning achievement.

The overall aim of the module

The aim of the module was 'to emphasize the importance of Temperature Control in the total operation of the units'.

Temperature control, along with personal hygiene and unit sanitation, incorporate the majority of hygiene precautions which must be stressed at all levels. Temperature levels are easier to recognize than the presence of bacteria but many operatives are vague about the importance of temperatures, or the need to actually check refrigeration-unit temperatures. Consequently, 'The module will therefore be designed to present a range of facts which will make operatives more aware of the hazards and precautions linked with temperature control.'

■ CPD MILESTONE 105 – THE RANGE OF OBJECTIVES APPLIED TO THE MODULE

Continuing with the Food Handling and Temperature Control module, after each of the following objectives, I have indicated the type/level. As an event outcome, the learner will be competent to:

1. Define the terminology applied, including 'food handling', 'temperature control' and 'temperature danger zone'. (Cognitive: Knowledge level)
2. Explain the implications and application of the temperature danger zone, as it applies to the cooking and storage of foodstuffs. (Cognitive: Comprehension/Application)
3. Discuss the different ranges applied in Celsius/Centigrade and Fahrenheit and identify which is used in each participant's country/unit. (Cognitive: Knowledge → Application)
4. Demonstrate the correct and safe use of the digital pyrometer for the monitoring of internal and external temperatures of foodstuffs in all areas. (The 'digital pyrometer' is an industrial thermometer with a LCD readout and a temperature-gauge probe (which must be sanitized between use).) (Psychomotor and Cognitive: Application → Analysis)
5. Check and monitor temperatures in the kitchen refrigerators, cold stores and holding cabinets, in order to establish conformity with company standards. (Psychomotor and Cognitive: Application)
6. Identify the key criteria for handling and storage of raw and cooked foodstuffs, with special reference to high-hazard goods. (Cognitive: Knowledge and Comprehension)
7. Consider methods of handling such hazardous foodstuffs to reduce bacterial counts to a minimum. (Cognitive: Application, with elements of Analysis and Synthesis)
8. Apply the knowledge learned in this module to carry out a kitchen temperature audit of your immediate workplace. (Psychomotor and Cognitive: → Evaluation level)

CONSIDERING THE DETAIL

The list above will be sufficient detail for the purpose of the exercise. Looking through these objectives, you should begin to identify the key information and the outcome which is required in each. The more you consider it, the more each objective flags the detail, criteria, equipment and technique required, indicating the information necessary.

USING OBJECTIVES TO ASSESS COMPLETION

Where we consider the objective wording in order to monitor its completion, we can extrapolate all manner of detail to help us judge the level of success. Remember that a complete objective – even a cognitive one – should include indications of action, conditions and standards expected, to allow us to evaluate progress and completion.

Examples

In Objective 4, for example, we would have to check that the learner could use all controls on the digital pyrometer to set it up for checking both internal and external temperatures of foodstuffs, while practising the hygiene precautions necessary. It is therefore more important to monitor the cognitive areas of the objective relating to hygiene – and to ensure that these standards are maintained – than to check achievement of the psychomotor equipment operation (which is an initial, ten-minute exercise). Extending further than this immediate training activity, the ongoing maintenance of this important hygiene standard relies on the availability of supplies of sterile wipes for the probe. Our triangular integration prompts Management/DSF to arrange for this supply.

In Objective 6, we would require reference to the criteria and standards in force in the kitchen, both through company documentation and Environmental Health Department guidelines. We would also need to identify what are considered as 'high-hazard' goods – and any special handling procedures which are associated with them. Thus, in terms of monitoring standards, this objective would relate to 'official' rules and regulations which must be known and observed. This ongoing requirement is not really 'training', but more the maintenance of a high level of awareness and vigilance.

It is hard enough, for example, to sustain motivation with airport security staff, where suspicious shapes show up on the scanner screen with some degree of regularity – kitchen staff can't *see* pathogenic bacteria on the food. Neither will they normally be aware of the effects of minor food poisoning as the bacteria often don't take effect for twenty or thirty hours, long after passengers have disembarked and dispersed. It is hard, therefore, to keep the potential effects of slipped standards uppermost in minds.

SUCCESSFUL MONITORING OF ACHIEVEMENT

The monitoring of achievement of this type of objective, therefore, is two-fold. At the outcome level, the learner must demonstrate awareness of the key criteria and competency at using temperature control as a physical and visible means of checking and maintaining hygiene standards. Learners must also demonstrate the attitude to maintain this vigilance consistently after the initial learning is complete, which must be monitored.

 ## CPD MILESTONE 106 – THE REAL VALUE OF USING OBJECTIVES

The more you consider an objective, the more detail, assessment criteria – and methods of application and completion – come to mind. Objectives may take time to compose initially but they become an extemely valuable reference point for all stages of the development, realization and evaluation which follow. I hope, by now, you agree!

So, at the stage of reviewing both progress and ultimate achievement, we can use the objective statements to identify:

O   standards to assess the degree of achievement of that particular development area;
O   the degree to which these have been achieved; and
O   particular elements which may require further effort.

 ## CPD MILESTONE 107 – REVIEWING PROGRESS: IS THE TEAMWORK WORKING?

Effective teamwork is a crucial element of this entire personal and professional development strategy. We can consider this teamwork at the level of getting people generally to think beyond assertion and towards co-operation. This leads in turn to genuine support for other learners in achieving their development initiatives – and forms the basis of growing mentoring involvement. It's the attitude shift which is important.

We also have the more immediate teamwork of our triangular integration and the assessment of how this three-way link is working. This includes the change in mind-set which we must achieve from training provider to DSF – and the company-wide implications of a sustained mentoring strategy. That's a lot of foundations to build, and test, to ensure that they are strong enough to support the rigours of further development.

 ## CPD MILESTONE 108 – REVIEWING THE FOUNDATIONS OF OUR TEAM BUILDING

The country road which runs past the Wiltshire house where I lived in southern England was originally a Saxon 'herepath' or warpath. Over marshy sections, this track was constructed by tying twigs together in bundles and laying these as foundations. Each twig was not very strong individually but, joined together, the bundle brought support. That's the importance of foundations – and that's the beneficial holistic effect of individuals working together in teams – reading off the same route map. How can we check that the team's 'map-reading uniformity' is improving? It's Route Review time.

ROUTE REVIEW 9

1_____10
LOW   HIGH

■ The concept of triangular integration is accepted throughout my department/the organization.

■ The Development Support Function has established its role and this is generally understood and accepted.

■ Individuals are involved in applying some form of development planning system, which is being used both as a reference and a monitoring device by others.

■ A mentoring strategy is in place, which is encouraging co-operative activities.

- Team meetings are occurring formally and informally to integrate individual skills for improved overall effect.

- Individuals are proactively involved in identifying their needs and establishing personal strategies to develop them.

- CPD recording is being achieved at a competency/outcome level, giving indications of subsequent, related activities.

- There is a genuine transition in place, involving more positive assertion, with some progression towards co-operation.

- There is a positive attitude towards the facilitation of a full range of learning events, with support for their consolidation.

HOW CAN THE EFFECTIVENESS OF THESE DEVELOP FURTHER?

REALISTIC SITUATIONS – REALISTIC EXPECTATIONS

We are seeking progress here – so don't expect the Earth. You can also assume that there will be glitches and setbacks in our team development, but this does not signify that the whole system cannot work. Think of any setback as merely a test to see whether the system is flexible enough. If you think 'bigger picture', it's surprising how unimportant many things really are. When viewed objectively, their true significance becomes clear.

Example

Before my wife became a writer, she was a self-employed systems analyst, and for some time she worked as a consultant with a water utility company on a new computerized billing system. She used to become very frustrated by some of the 'brick walls', both computer- and people-related. I had to remind her periodically that, in the end, it was just a water bill . . .

It's very easy, when working very close to some project over an extended period of time, to lose a sense of perspective. It's only when we exist in that mind-set that problems appear insurmountable, innocent comments become slights threatening to blast the team cohesion apart, and negative attitudes then kick in.

When some misfortune threatens, consider seriously and deliberately what is the very worst that could possibly happen.
Having looked this possible misfortune in the face, give yourself sound reasons for thinking that after all it would be no such terrible disaster.
Such reasons always exist, since at the worst nothing that happens to oneself has any cosmic importance.

Bertrand Russell, *The Conquest of Happiness*,
George Allen & Unwin, 1975

It's important to stand back from things periodically in order to see the bigger picture. Remember the benefit of removing yourself to a higher vantage point to survey the developmental track. This allows you to view overall progress more objectively. Before we complete this review, I would like to reinforce one previous point again.

CPD MILESTONE 109 – MAINTAINING PROGRESS TOWARDS CO-OPERATION

We have considered the logical progression from *belonging*, through *assertion* to *co-operation* in several different scenarios. We have concentrated primarily on the transition between *assertion* and *co-operation*: I would like to underline that it is just that – a transition – rather than some 'flash-of-inspiration' shift of consciousness.

As with all interactions, the presence of two or more parties in any group or team creates dynamic movement, like swirling eddies. We must respond to these in an equally dynamic, living way. The waging of modern warfare, complete with media circus, remote discussion and focus groups and parallel political agendas, is a good example of the ever-changing transition between assertion and co-operation. Where this involves the co-ordination of a multinational policing role within a country such as the former Yugoslavia, riven by its own internal divisions, a study of the attempts to elicit co-operation has valuable spin-off lessons for negotiating in the business world.

ADAPTING THE RESPONSE TO REVIEW AND MAINTAIN PROGRESS

Even though we acknowledge this progress from assertion to co-operation, we must also accept the need when reviewing, to 'regress' to applying assertive responses on occasion, in order to unblock stalemate situations. I do not consider this to be necessarily lowering standards, but merely responding to the dynamics of the situation.

Perhaps I can propose the benefits of prevention rather than cure, on occasion. Reviewing any situation from a co-operative viewpoint, we can possibly see a solution which will help everyone in the end, although undoubtedly requiring compromise. If we can assert this solution – or more likely some concession agreement – on others, we may 'nip the crisis in the bud' and progress to more co-operative interactions once more.

Example

I was brought up in a village in Scotland in an era when the village policeman spent a lot of his time chatting to people on street corners. He therefore heard on the grapevine if Malcolm was planning a little bit of house-breaking or Hamish was driving an untaxed and uninsured vehicle. A quiet but assertive word in Hamish's ear and an assertive 'clip' round Malcolm's – and the co-operative status quo in the village returned.

We may need to apply more politically correct methods nowadays but prevention is often a lot faster – and usually cheaper – than cure. Meeting assertion with assertion in an open, responsive manner (as in defensive, though assured, driving rather than road rage) can often lead to a preventative solution, if approached objectively and laterally.

THE PROBLEMS IN ATTAINING UNIVERSAL CO-OPERATION

It is important to stress that we must always be consciously trying to progress towards reaching compromise agreed by *all* parties. There is little long-term mileage in forcing through agreements where one party is evidently disadvantaged – and probably incapable of enforcing the 'agreement' on their membership. This is especially true with individuals who are still thinking and acting in assertive mode. Any acceptance cannot really be expected to last, without maintained imposition, which is a false dawn.

We can probably think of recent political 'settlements' where deadlines have been made for the acceptance of imposed agreements. History is speckled with such examples, with recent diplomacy in

Northern Ireland and the Balkans or the presence of permanent peace-keeping forces as living examples to encourage great caution in our business and life negotiations. History's value extends beyond passing examinations.

 ## CPD MILESTONE 110 – REVIEWING PROGRAMMES AND MATERIALS

Before we complete our review of progress, we must consider how we are managing to respond to the need for a wide range of learning materials, programmes and other solutions being available to respond to detailed shortfall analysis at individual level.

This highlights another valuable use of objectives – in checking the validity of materials and programmes. It is very easy to be distracted by the immediate impact or the exciting technology of an interactive video, a residential course or conference abroad, or other programmes where the activity's attractiveness may overshadow the outcome.

Obviously, learning with a bit of glamour or excitement attached is a plus, *as long as* the published programme/material objectives meet the individual's analysed learning objectives as closely as possible. Although one can scan a text programme quite quickly to get a feel for its appropriateness, it is harder to check the validity of something interactive such as CBT or interactive video, where the quality of the interactivity may be the issue. You have to check the programme in real time, by actually using it.

Applying these objectives-based techniques, we can both review the content of existing and customized programmes and materials – and ensure that we build the range of modules available as rapidly as possible. Any move towards responding to development at an individual level will be highly dependent on this ever-widening range of responses.

ESTABLISHING REFERENCE REVIEWS OF RESOURCE EFFECTIVENESS

It is valuable, when you have some form of resource or learning centre, to have filed written reviews of the materials and programmes on the shelves. These reviews will cover areas such as objectives, content, quality of interaction and consolidation, levels, relationship with other learning materials available, and so on. These are certainly time-consuming to produce, but once filed, they act as a valuable reference for subsequent users, if there is no knowledgeable mentor or DSF staff member available.

CPD MILESTONE 111 – MONITORING PROGRESS THROUGH COMPETENCY TESTING

If we can expend more effort on establishing and validating real levels of competency testing, we could compare and contrast individual achievement more scientifically, providing a more standardized reference point. Detailed competency levels will permit more direct comparison between individual CPD records. There have certainly been a variety of attempts at specifying levels and ranges for specific occupations and professions. I would say, however, that these lack overall co-ordination at an appropriate intellectual and authoritative level, which is impeding acceptance and implementation.

CPD MILESTONE 112 – REVIEWING THE REVIEW PROCESS!

It is important to review progress regularly, in order to maintain an objective viewpoint and to ensure that the individual paths are still moving forward confidently within the track parameters. The expression 'lifelong learning' is used now to underscore the need for continuity and progression, encouraging individuals to update current skills and learn new ones which are relevant to their perceived direction of development.

Keeping a close watch on this development, through the planning and monitoring process of a good CPD system, will help the individual maintain a view of ongoing progress and retain high motivational levels. It will also allow individuals to drive the whole process forward, with a little help from their friends in the integrated triangle.

KEEPING OUR EYE ON THE GOAL

Milestones were very important to stagecoach travellers of old, lacking the benefits of tachographs and odometers. Taken in the context of a three-day journey from Portsmouth to London, the visible passage of every mile becomes a highly motivating event, relatively speaking, bearing in mind the hard seating and lack of leaf springs!

 CPD MILESTONE 113 – CPD MILESTONES

Milestones, as we're all aware, relate to distance along an established road or track. Thus, we have our monitoring indicators at regular intervals along the development track. But then we've also established that each individual path is a meander along the track – although the linear distance is still measured by the indicators, the actual journey (or individual effort expended between indicators) will often be greater.

THE NEED FOR ADDITIONAL MILESTONES

As our CPD path is evolving, in distance or expended effort terms, we are in effect creating additional milestones for ourselves. Sometimes, this merely means that we are travelling six miles to traverse a linear distance of five. At other times, we are creating additional sub-goals or objectives in order to ultimately achieve the main goal or milestone. Initial planning, therefore, gives us our individual goals and plan of action – our route plan. Conscious triangular integration ensures that the whole caravan moves forward as effectively as possible, towards an acceptable holistic outcome.

Example

I worked on a project once where I was part of a team involved in producing training for a new IT system scheduled to 'go live' on a particular date. Project planning then established the milestones stretching backwards from the end goal: for training to commence, materials and programmes developed, operational guides written, new system integrated and tested, roles stipulated, new system installed, and so on.

Of course, in the project plan, this meant that many of the earlier milestones or goals were months away from the end date. Training, on the other hand, started only about a fortnight before 'going live', with a packed schedule to cover all necessary competencies.

In project planning, critical paths and so on, the whole point is to establish that there is a path with critical deadlines throughout. It does not matter whether a particular milestone is two years, two months or two weeks before the final 'go live' date – it is crucial that each deadline on that critical path is met, within the parameters stated, otherwise the overall project cannot succeed on schedule.

The demise of the project plan

Because of management and organizational failure, the triangular structure in this project broke down, with the inevitable stress and last-minute 'seat-of-the-pants' flying. And so the world will tend to be: with much of the stress relating to work pressures caused by the actions of those above, who should be equally involved in development planning, milestoning and monitoring overall progress. Some people get an adrenalin rush from working in this chaos – I feel a frustrated anger that it need not be happening. As the holistic atmosphere spreads, I dream that it will spread into boardrooms, enlightening both involvement and purpose – and kicking sense into those who should know better!

 ## CPD MILESTONE 114 – PLANNING AN INDIVIDUAL CPD PROJECT

CPD scheduling is also a form of project planning. Some of it will be less time-critical, while some will require regular review and rescheduling to keep it moving forward. But regular monitoring by each individual will keep tabs on the completion of actions which are necessary to keep their development progressing.

Consider the following:

○   Which of my planned activities will require approval for financial allocation?
○   Do I need to book ahead for some future activities or resources?
○   Have I 'bitten off more than I can chew', in setting some of my milestones/objectives? Might these benefit by subdivision?
○   Are the standards against which I can monitor progress and success still clear?
○   Would it be helpful to liaise with others following similar paths for specific subjects?
○   Can I combine and integrate some of my personal and professional development?
○   Have my needs priorities shifted since originally planning my current CPD path?
○   Am I still finding opportunities to reinforce the outcomes of previous learning?
○   Where there's a logical cognitive flow (knowledge → evaluation), is this happening?
○   Is there anything I need to do to improve the support from my integrated triangle?
○   Is there anything I need to do to improve my individual planning and monitoring?
○   Do I need to review and revise the structure of the system I am using, in order that it works effectively to satisfy my needs, priorities and preferred development methods?

TIME OUT

There's a lot to think about in the above individual action list. Have you managed to develop your own CPD planning and recording system to some extent? Do you feel empowered and involved enough in your own development plans to review *your* progress?

CPD MILESTONE 115 – REPOSITIONING THE MILESTONES

We've been speaking about the 'goalposts shifting' in a fairly negative way, within the context of someone else shifting them as you take aim to shoot. If you are a parent, you will have met the 'but you promised' scenario. If you promise a child that you'll do something, disappointment and tears will ensue if it does not occur exactly as defined, regardless of any changes between statement and expected outcome. I like to think that adults function more maturely, although this is by no means always the case!

Sometimes, in the cold light of reality or necessity, the need to change plans becomes imperative – goalposts are moved or milestones shifted in a more considered, reasoned manner. We must be aware, however, that any reasonableness in our mind justifying the plan change may not be quite so apparent to the child or to a learner expecting CPD activities. Here, we have another case where effort must be put into refining or changing attitudes in order to allow progress to continue. In objective terms, we are 'achieving affective/ attitudinal change before we attempt cognitive input'.

CPD MILESTONE 116 – ADDING EXTRA MILESTONES TO MEET DETAILED NEEDS

When we consider a particular development need, we often see the additional detail – those extra milestones of complexity – gradually appearing as we progressively delve more deeply into the situation. In visual terms, we have the 'normal' learning stages represented by the main, regular milestones, with the supplementary input (which might be necessary remedial studies, specialist knowledge required by the individual, and so on) indicated by the 'add-on extra' milestones along the learner's meandering path.

CPD MILESTONE 117 – CASE STUDY

Let's spend some time considering John's communication problem. John is a middle-aged, middle manager who is good at his job and skilled at applying the advanced techniques within his portfolio. He is however poor at explaining clearly what he is doing to others – and becomes outwardly frustrated at their apparent stupidity when they do not understand. He uses his computer satisfactorily when it suits him, but dislikes any interactive computer techniques, such as e-mail. As his department is remote from head office, the company has recently installed video conferencing facilities, which John hates. His writing skills are very good. As a manager, he keeps his staff informed individually but steers clear of larger meetings or public statements.

TIME OUT

Write down some of John's key communication shortfalls – and initial ideas of how you might respond. You can compare your ideas with those which follow later in this case study.

ESTABLISHING SPECIFIC SHORTFALL DETAIL

You have created information for John's CPD planning, highlighting his main 'Competency Shortfall Area' under the particular target area of 'Communication'. If you look back at CPD Milestone 56, you will see that 'Areas of competency shortfall' was one of the potential headings for our overall CPD planning system.

In John's case, 'Communication' would undoubtedly subdivide further into areas of 'verbal' and 'technology' – we will focus on the verbal side, for the purpose of this exercise.

ANALYSING SHORTFALLS AND POSSIBLE RESPONSES

Using the appropriate format headings, John's competency shortfalls may be noted as shown on the following page, set out as it might appear in one of our CPD format sheets. Study this now.

IDENTIFYING THE IN-DEPTH RESPONSES – THE EXTRA MILESTONES

If you refer once more to the suggested headings in CPD Milestone 56, applying the planning system allows us to progress further to:

○ considering all target areas and prioritizing them;
○ refining the action statements into full objectives statements;
○ identifying possible learning techniques and resources which might be applied;
○ establishing a total sequence of milestones to advance through in order to ultimately reach the goal specified in the overall objective statement (the CPD plan);

COMPETENCY SHORTFALL AREAS

TARGET AREA: Communication – Verbal

COMPETENCY SHORTFALL – DETAIL

1. Using cognitive levels to make explanations progress clearly and logically.
2. Identifying target audience (listener) levels.
3. Using listening skills to establish levels of understanding.
4. Presenting information to meetings.
5. Presenting information to static camera.

INITIAL RESPONSE CONCEPTS

1. Establish different basic levels – and indicators of each.
   Practise examples of delivering information progressively.

2. Apply different cognitive levels to expected listener levels.
   Discuss expectations of different listeners.
   Analyse methods of getting the message across to different listeners.

3. Consider questioning technique – and relate to expected learner levels.
   Practise identifying detail from statements.
   Practise listening and responding to statements and questions.

4. Review the establishment of clear objectives statements.
   Consider basic meetings presentation skills.
   Establish benefits of making precise summary statements.
   Practise listening and responding to questions positively.
   Practise pitching statements at established listener levels and types.

5. Relate presentation and listening skills learned in (4) to video conferencing.
   Practise techniques of talking to camera and involving specific listeners.
   Discuss the limitations of fixed camera work and establish best practice.
   Establish the importance of discussion co-ordination and management.

RELATED CONSIDERATIONS

1. IT – internal communication devices: e-mail (plus any others necessary) technical operation and applications (written communication skills – OK competence).
2. IT – external communication devices: video conferencing (plus any others) technical operation and applications (link with camera communication skills).

○ considering additional inputs required to meet John's particular shortfalls; and finally

○ reviewing methods of monitoring and assessing their overall achievement.

At this stage in our analysis, however, we are considering the foundations necessary to establish John's initial competency areas and select potential techniques which we can apply to overcome his identified blocks (some of which may be unique to him).

In real terms, therefore, John might be placed on an open-access Communication Skills course selected to meet as many of his objectives as possible. His additional needs (extra milestones) would then be satisfied by particular modules, mentoring and so on.

JOHN'S POTENTIAL RESPONSES

If you look at the initial ideas which are detailed as 'Response Concepts' in the Competency Shortfall Area sheet, you should see a logical sequence for charting progress:

○ Learn the cognitive levels, as they apply to getting information across at meetings.

○ Apply these in basic practical examples.

○ Analyse listener levels.

○ Apply the implications of using the cognitive sequence for different listener levels.

○ Consider different ways of getting the message across.

○ Consider ways, such as effective questioning, of developing two-way communication.

○ Using objective statements, identify ways of maintaining clear focus on goals.

○ Review basic presentation skills, with reference to discussion leading in meetings.

○ Apply this knowledge to the slightly different skills of video conferencing.

 CPD MILESTONE 118 – SPOTTING THE POTENTIAL BLOCKAGES

Let's take the sequence of John's potential responses, set out above, as our initially planned sequence for his CPD. Through this, he can

respond to his communication shortfalls in a logical progression, taking time to reinforce each learning stage with on-the-job practice as necessary. Have a look at the sequence again – and check back to review our initial statement of John's shortfall. Can you spot any potential blocks?

Consider the following:

O   What about John's initial attitudes towards speaking publicly?
O   Can we isolate the technology aspect or could it become an over-whelming factor?
O   Will he be able to accept the need for the structured, analytical approach?
O   How can we get him involved in the practical exercises necessary to 'sell the ideas'?
O   Is there an inter-personal relationship problem with his staff which will have to be addressed first, to allow his application practice to be more successful?
O   Are there any external factors which might prevent him developing these areas?

■ CPD MILESTONE 119 – POSSIBLE RESPONSES TO MEET IDENTIFIED NEEDS

The first key task would be to help John sort out any attitudinal problems. Why is he uncomfortable when talking to his staff? Has he ever figured out why people fail to understand the detail he is telling them? Does he listen to what people are saying? Then there's the technology blockage. It's not our major focus at the moment, but it will be there as a background consideration, so may rise to the surface periodically.

He'll probably have problems coming to terms with listener levels – and accepting that he needs to direct his message differently to different people. This is especially true as he probably believes that lack of understanding or acceptance is caused by stupidity on the part of the listener and is nothing to do with the quality or content of his message.

We will have to change the attitude first, and then focus on the subdivision of levels and their application. This is not necessarily a block but it could take time to sort out.

THE IMPORTANCE OF COMMUNICATION AS A TWO-WAY PROCESS

We can perhaps sell the two-way communication concept to John by putting him in the position of being a learner – of finding out how to practise some completely new skill – through applying a sequence of questions and answers. We will, of course, have to reinforce the message at the end that *he* can then apply this when leading a discussion, in order to improve his two-way communication. After all, he sounds like someone who can spot deficiencies in others but considers his own technique to be faultless ... but then perhaps we're all a bit like that!

With this and with the various areas where he will be applying his newly-learned communication skills in meetings and the video-conferencing suite, he will need to be mentored discreetly and sympathetically. This is by no means a block, but will need a time commitment from both him and his mentor(s) over an extended period. Time availability is often a problem – we may have to help him manage his time better.

 ## CPD MILESTONE 120 – CHARTING THE LONGER PATH, WITH ADDED MILESTONES

In real life, this study would go much deeper but we have probed enough to see how John's development needs will progressively expand. From having an initial 'communication problem' which might traditionally have been resolved (to some extent, at least) by sending John on a Communications Skills course, we now see that his path is much more complex and unique, requiring individually-designed responses. Through a close consideration of:

○   his particular shortfall areas;
○   the cognitive sequence which he should follow;
○   his priorities, to effect a rapid and visible improvement;
○   the implications of the various specific blocks which he might experience; and
○   the preferred solutions and techniques which allow him to move forward,

John, in association with his manager/mentor and with support from the DSF, can establish his preferred development programme, to be set down in his CPD system.

GETTING EVERYONE INVOLVED IN THE PROCESS

It is quite possible that John – and his manager – have had little experience of thinking objectively, certainly within a training and development context. Thus, training John in concepts such as Cognitive Sequencing is part of the initial 'CPD induction' and attitudinal input which will be required to get the whole thing moving positively.

We do not want the DSF corner of our integrated triangle to be the only 'specialists' who know how to compose development objectives. The degree of empowerment, involvement and motivation which we are seeking to instill in all parties means that they *all* need to be reading from the same route map. The depth of understanding can obviously vary in the different corners – with the DSF the ultimate driving force – but the overall understanding must be present to allow open and progressive negotiations.

Before we consider this further, let's check on some of John's areas which *you* might have to advance for your *own* development planning.

ROUTE REVIEW 10

```
1_____10
LOW    HIGH
```

■   The CPD planning system is used universally as a reference point by all parties in the integrated triangle.

■   Planning and the realization of development plans are seen in flexible terms, with amendment possible where justifiable.

■   My own individual development plan is well advanced and reflects many of my agreed priority areas.

■   I can see the way ahead with my development – and am consciously considering any blocks which might occur.

■   I am getting the opportunities to apply and reinforce my on-the-job learning, with mentored remedial help as needed.

■ I feel confident to adapt the CPD planning system I am using to apply it more closely to my personal needs and priorities.

WHICH OF THE ABOVE ARE PRIORITIES FOR FURTHER ACTION?

 ## CPD MILESTONE 121 – NEGOTIATING TO KEEP MOVING

Negotiation will often involve the cross-over point between co-operation and assertion – with the key challenge being to get the correct mix. You are probably well aware of the win–win style in negotiation, where both parties feel that they have won some concluding agreement. With no 'loss of face', everyone feels that they have reached a satisfactory outcome and relationships are cemented for future co-operation.

As with our earlier communication examples, which sometimes require a change from co-operative to assertive reactions, negotiation will also require this shift, when dealing with more assertive behaviour (to move a win–lose to a win–win and leave everyone thinking positively). Two negotiators acting co-operatively will, of course, also reach a win–win conclusion, usually more speedily and with a lot less angst.

'I'M BIGGER THAN YOU, SO JUST WATCH OUT!'

Rank-pulling would seem to me to be one of the biggest blocks – and the most opaque hidden agenda – existing in the business world, especially when it is used as an overriding response to what is in effect poor management and planning. It often happens as a chain reaction, with bucks being passed down the line and crisis responses requested within ridiculous timescales. This, of course, causes knock-on chaos to everyone else's planned schedules – but then 'they're only subordinates'.

How many of us have been asked to re-prioritize workloads or to work late at some point to complete a report/produce a letter/create some presentation visuals for a boss? As an independent consultant, I have had many demands for presentation 'rush jobs' to be produced overnight and couriered to offices, ready for use in meetings. It was always possible, of course, but I found that the high additional 'priority fees' charged by many production studios helped encourage better planning for future assignments!

 ## CPD MILESTONE 122 – POSITIVE NEGOTIATION STRATEGIES

Without preaching anarchy here, sometimes being assertive is the only way of setting the parameters which ensure that reasonable timescales are allocated and adequate warning given. Take the case of the bad planner who has to face up to the consequences of not having the materials to hand for her presentation. For once, it was collectively not possible for anyone to work into the night to produce her visuals. You can guarantee that she will put a little more fore-thought and planning into her next requirement. Meet assertion with assertion, politely and calmly.

You could try responses such as:

○ 'You have already asked for responses to these three activities for tonight. If you want me to do this new one, how do you prioritize the four – and which one will be OK if left until tomorrow?'
○ 'I'm working on this project for Mr Barrington at the moment – could you have a word with him to sort out priorities and get back to me?'

Sometimes, you must compromise on that occasion, while setting the guidelines for the amount of warning required in the future. This gives a reference point for the next time.

KEEPING YOUR EYE ON THE NEGOTIATION GOAL

Negotiation, with a win–win goal in mind, should be conducted in a civilized manner, reducing any potential imbalance created by status or rank:

A: 'Would it be possible for me to have some development on Customer Care?'
B: 'What do you need that for?'
A: 'I feel that it would help me respond better to the real needs of the customer.'
B: 'We don't have the budget to send you on a course – maybe next financial year.'

A: 'I don't necessarily have to go on a course – but I need the development now.'

B: 'There isn't the time, unless you do it in your own time.'

A: 'With all the additional time I've worked over the last year, I feel that the company could give me some time to study within the working day.'

B: 'What – you mean an afternoon?'

A: 'Not necessarily even a full afternoon. I can slot in study time for an hour or so in the quieter times, if the company can provide self-learn materials.'

B: 'Does the DSF have any at the moment?'

A: 'They have some but there's a particular package I would like to study. It would be a good one to have in the resources bank though – lots of people could use it.'

B: 'Well, as long as it's not too expensive, that should be possible, I suppose. And you don't need to go on a course?'

A: 'No. It would help if I had someone who would act as mentor to talk things through . . .'

Keeping an eye on your goal and priorities during negotiation will help to keep you moving forward; concede what you do not consider important but use compromise concessions as stepping stones to push for the issues which *are* important to you.

 ## CPD MILESTONE 123 – KEEPING THE PACE GOING

As we have established from a variety of angles, once the concept of individual development takes off in an organization, the challenge for the DSF is to respond to the increased needs and requests – to provide the supply in order to meet the demand. There are various roles which we have already considered, such as:

○ Identify key needs priorities and respond to these first.

○ Produce programmes which will meet the needs of a wide target population.

○ Consider the inclusion of 'low-tech' responses as a wider-reaching solution.

○ Develop coaching and mentoring support as a flexible resource.

○ Build an effective triangular infrastructure to maintain communication links.

○ Consider a modular approach, to allow maximum flexibility.

○ Maintain effective monitoring through an active CPD planning/recording system.

○   Use holistic team and co-operative strategies to keep the programme progressing.

The DSF has a very valuable role to play in all this, acting not only
as provider and facilitator, but also as the responsible corner of the
triangle which is in the strongest position to keep sight of the 'bigger
picture'.

Visualize our high-vantage viewing point over the CPD track, sur-
veying the intertwining threads of the many individual development
paths. Looking closely, we can see a tiny figure – representing an
individual learner – at the head of each path. Note the glints of blue
from the mentor's armbands worn by many – the holistic effect is
working!

We can also visualize the figures of DSF members, mingling with
the individual learners. Because of its origins, the DSF is still seen
as the driving force for development, which is to be expected. When
we get to areas of needs analysis, priority identification, techniques
selection, individual CPD programme scheduling and monitoring –
areas where we are down at the individual level of response – we have
the situation where the individuals and manager/mentors are now
involved. Training, help and support will be provided, of course . . .
bringing in the DSF once again and thus completing the triangle.

CPD MILESTONE 124 – THE VALUABLE NEW ROLE OF THE DSF

The DSF's role involves getting out and about meeting people, being
seen as an internal consultant, there to build customized responses
(which need not be a course), and displaying a knowledge of the range
of responses possible – and the objectivity to select the most appropriate ones to suit the individual rather than the department's
convenience.

It is a real challenge – but an exciting one. Traditionally, we elaborate at great length in Customer Services training courses about the
'internal customer'. We advocate working with them and responding
to their needs in much the same way as we deal with the normal
'external' customer. The individual learner is the key 'internal customer' for the DSF – so we must practise what we preach!

THE POTENTIAL FOR SHORT-TERM SUPPORT

I would also like to draw attention to a vast resource of freelance training professionals who are potentially available to give this development support. As another piece of lateral thinking for DSFs, consider buying these people in on a daily basis to apply their wide-ranging experience.

You can probably negotiate design and development day rates which are less than the price you'd pay to send someone on a public course for the day – and you'll get more value added at the end of it. Think beyond merely having courses run by these independents: consider them more as a potential extra pair of design, development and organizational hands. Respect experience – they're very keen to become involved.

TIME OUT FOR REST AND REFLECTION

We have covered many different aspects for keeping our eye on the goal and ensuring that progress can continue unrestricted. Much of this is focused on the individual's professional development and how this is managed within the business environment.

As we pause for a rest break on our route progress down the track, there's time to reflect on the individual's – and your own – personal development and how this can be progressed further.

XI

CHARACTER BUILDING

Each player must accept the cards life deals him or her.
But once they are in hand, he or she alone must decide how to
play the cards, in order to win the game

Voltaire

Faith, trust, empowerment, self-belief, confidence, self-awareness, actualization – call it what you will – we should all believe that we individually have this little spark of energy inside us which can ignite the flame of progress and development.

 ## CPD MILESTONE 125 – ESTABLISHING OUR PERSONAL PARAMETERS

Visualizing our track with its spaghetti of intertwining paths once more, these – and the little figure we can see at the head of each path – represent individual development in action. We have been tending to relate the boundaries of this track to business criteria, but the overall composition is of course more complex than this. Our ultimate path is bounded by moral and ethical standards, laws and regulations and the myriad of personal standards we apply to our lives. Many of these are variable; for example, when is theft theft? Is taking some paper clips and a ballpoint pen home from work theft? Is helping yourself to a cake from the tin in the kitchen? Is eating one or two sweets from the supermarket 'pick and mix'? Is taking a bar of chocolate, without paying?

Ultimately, we individually write the 'small print' in our life contract to a detail which is acceptable to us – creating the parameters for our personal development. This is what makes each individual unique.

My wife and I brought up our two children to understand the parameters within which we live, but if you study us as four beings, we each live by slightly different personal standards – with different priorities, different concepts of right and wrong and of what is considered acceptable and not acceptable. It is probably much the same with most families. It makes the facilitation of personal development a more complex activity – but infinitely more interesting!

CPD MILESTONE 126 – FOCUS ON PERSONAL DEVELOPMENT

So far, our consideration of the individual has been focused within the context of professional development and how the individual integrates with the DSF and the mentors in our business triangle. In this chapter, we concentrate on *personal* development: how each individual can work on self-improvement, enlightenment, altruism, community spirit, leading a religious/spiritual/etc. way of life, selflessness – as long as the description feels right for that individual, use it. We are concerned here not with one belief system over another, but with self-improvement integrating with the overall betterment of society. The application is equally relevant to all corners of our integrated business triangle – as it potentially involves us all.

I have used the term *holistic* in a variety of contexts, where the final outcome is more valuable and effective than the sum of its components. Many of the examples have illustrated the holistic effect of individuals acting for the common good rather than for overriding personal gain, generating a fusion of team spirit. This is to be desired.

CPD MILESTONE 127 – PERSONAL DEVELOPMENT AND THE SPIRITUAL

It's difficult to define in real terms exactly what is encapsulated in living a more 'spiritual' way of life. The Oxford English Dictionary defines spiritual as 'having the higher qualities of the mind; concerned with or based on the spirit'. Exponents of each religious faith may consider spirituality to be uniquely their own; some read into it the threat of what they see as the black arts of the paranormal; some equate it with 'New Age' or even pagan concepts. I am not concerned here with any debate about 'anyone's God being better than anyone else's God' – indeed, in energy terms I consider it all to be one and the same. Instead, we will focus on how the act of aspiring to what we would term a holistic way of life can influence personal development both directly and indirectly.

EXPANDING YOUR VIEW OF MIND, BODY AND SPIRIT

Since the mid-1990s, there has certainly been an increased interest in 'Mind, Body and Spirit' matters. Because of this, there is now a wide range of published literature discussing aspects of living a more spiritual or holistic way of life – and many courses and other forms of retreat which can be attended. I find that advocates and practitioners of the many alternative therapies and stress-relieving techniques tend towards this way of thinking, again to varying degrees. If you have an interest in finding out more – or meeting like-minded souls to discuss your personal development thoughts on a spiritual plane – alternative therapists (or the local health food shop) are a good starting point. We have 'horses for courses', once again; as long as the effects and outcomes are considered and applied honestly and openly, the vehicle used is unimportant.

CPD MILESTONE 128 – LIVING A MORE HOLISTIC WAY OF LIFE

Although many might disagree, to me the beauty of the 'spiritual way of life' is that it provides a fairly open-ended framework against which you can personally test and fit your ideas. It also encourages selfless thinking and the neutralizing of the ego. Because of this open-endedness, I find that the objective, non-judgemental viewing of self and others is a major part of the development process.

Consider the following:

○ Do I agree to requests to help others without the 'what's in it for me?' question?
○ Do I involve myself in the community?
○ Am I conscious of my neighbours and keep an eye on their property as well as mine?
○ Do I consciously listen to what people are saying and respond to implied requests?
○ Do I offer help to people who might have basic needs (lifting cases, crossing roads)?

○ Do I offer encouragement to people who are expressing new plans and ideas?

○ Do I find time willingly within my own schedule to respond to requests from others?

○ Do I lend or give possessions which others would benefit from using?

○ Do I attempt to generate a positive, happy atmosphere for myself and others?

○ Do I attempt to generate an environment where people can feel comfortable?

These are some of the criteria we are working to achieve when developing towards living a holistic way of life. There will be lapses and there will be some areas which we find easier to apply than others ... but they give us a personal goal on which to focus. It is probably safe to say that we will never attain this overall goal – it is right off the end of our track and jetting towards enlightenment or Godliness, but these seem like good standards to aspire towards, however far back along this track we find ourselves!

> *Cease struggling and fighting*
> *Cease trying too hard*
> *and learn to let go*

> Eileen Caddy, *The Dawn of Change*,
> Findhorn Press, 1993

TIME OUT

As a cross-referencing exercise, spend a moment or two considering these criteria for personal development within a holistic way of life which are listed above. How might you integrate some of them with your professional development in the work environment?

 CPD MILESTONE 129 – HOLISTIC INVOLVEMENT IN THE COMMUNITY

Community spirit used to be a natural thing, in city or country. It still sends a shudder down my spine when I read of someone being discovered who has been lying dead for several months without the neighbours having noticed. Do we all interact positively with our neighbours on a regular basis? That seems like involvement in the community at the most basic level. Don't wait to be asked, though – do it because you feel you want to.

Be active in local clubs, schools and other groups trying to improve the life and ambience of the surrounding area. Offer help, informal or formal, to your local school. Join the committee of any group or establishment which genuinely interests you – and willingly bring your skills to improve its effectiveness. Don't just be a sleeping partner – *do* something.

THE RIGHT STUFF – THE RIGHT MOTIVES

There's no question that these types of activity look good on your CV and CPD records, but the key issue is that they broaden your development and attitudes while at the same time helping others. You will find that, as well as becoming more aware of the immediate world around you, your 'person' develops and you function on a broader plane. This improvement, once achieved, will have knock-on effects on your work, as well as on your life generally.

THE SYNERGY OF HOLISTIC INTERACTION

As we have established by now, there is a synergy between personal and professional development, so applying some of our learned business skills within our community activities will benefit the committee or club involved. The broader experience we gain from working alongside a variety of people in new environments and adapting our skills accordingly will help us refine and expand our lateral and objective thinking at work.

CPD MILESTONE 130 – THINKING AND ACTING CO-OPERATIVELY

Co-operation and the interaction between it and assertion has been an ongoing theme throughout this book. It is undoubtedly hard to achieve but is perhaps easier to experiment with in general life, where hidden agendas are less life- or job-threatening!

Example

In the last few years, I agreed on two separate occasions to be editor/producer of a local interest magazine/newsletter. This involved the full range of writing copy as well as editing, extending to final production – it was a very time-consuming exercise. I agreed with the concept and had some free time available, so I accepted the role. In both cases, however, having produced the monthly magazine for around a year, I found the lack of support and the pressures on my editorial integrity so heavy that I felt the atmosphere of co-operation, as well as fun and enjoyment, had disappeared.

In a business context, in what might have been one of my established responsibilities, withdrawal would have been difficult. As a social and voluntary activity, however, I could discuss the problems with 'management' and, where no solution was apparent, politely retire and concentrate my skills elsewhere. The experience was as valuable to me as was the end-product to them, however, and I have since applied my editorial and copy-writing skills elsewhere – so development certainly resulted from involvement.

CPD MILESTONE 131 – CO-OPERATION WITHIN PERSONAL DEVELOPMENT

As the saying goes: 'it takes two to tango.' It also takes two to co-operate. We have already considered the different permutations of co-operative/assertive interactions within a business context – we can perhaps apply them more freely in general life.

One problem I have come across in many different variations is the situation of having one's co-operative or helpful acts taken for granted. Perhaps you've experienced similar scenarios – you give a neighbour a lift to church every Sunday, only to find yourself being criticized for 'letting her down' on the one Sunday that you can't. It then becomes very hard to 'turn the other cheek'.

Example

I remember learning this lesson quite early in life, when I was a Scout. Every year, on parents' visiting day at Scout camp, my parents brought an insulated container of real ice cream and everyone had a large cone. One year, for whatever reason, my parents brought a box of bags of crisps instead. That evening, round the campfire, I listened to criticism about how mean my parents were, for not bringing the ice cream! However holistic or altruistic one is trying to be, co-operative activities do benefit from positive feedback to maintain the momentum – even no feedback is more motivating than negative feedback, in the cold reality of life!

Using this positively as a learning point, I see the value of varying the frequency of doing good deeds, so that people do not come to expect them, taking them for granted. When a good turn becomes a chore because of these negative attitudes, it is time to move to your high vantage point and visualize the bigger picture. By moving the goalposts for positive reasons, we encourage others to think more co-operatively.

 ## CPD MILESTONE 132 – 'DO ME A FAVOUR'

When someone says to you 'Can I ask a favour from you?', what is your immediate reply? Is it an immediate 'Yes' or is it a more hesitant 'It depends'? Does it depend to some extent on who's asking the favour? Sometimes it does. Indeed, should you agree to doing something without knowing what it is? Perhaps it's a commitment in principle at that stage – you are still at liberty to offer help to the extent you feel capable without necessarily obligating yourself totally. It is you who is doing the favour, after all, and they are at liberty to refuse your assistance and try elsewhere. A willingness to help others – to act co-operatively – is certainly one of our benchmarks.

 ## CPD MILESTONE 133 – THE MENTOR OVER THE GARDEN FENCE

The whole concept of mentoring and coaching is based on this attitude of co-operation. Gone is the concept of any form of training being the sole domain of trainers, with the direct involvement of other 'non-professionals' declined as being inappropriate.

Mentoring is by no means confined to business – in fact, it probably has its roots in personal development. What was your parents' role through your formative years? If a mentor is someone who has a specific skill or knowledge and who imparts this in an organized way to someone who does not, then informal mentoring has been going on in backyards for longer than you or I can remember. Picture the following scene:

John: 'You know about strimmers, don't you Bob. Why can't I get this one to run properly?'

Bob: 'Bring it over here and we'll have a look at it. Are you priming it first?'

John: 'Priming? I didn't know you had to prime it. How do you do that?'

And so the mentoring/coaching session proceeds. Visit the municipal parks on a Sunday and you'll find countless 'coaches' with their amateur child and adult football teams. In all probability, very few of them have had any formal training in coaching skills, but the valuable advice and assistance given to their prodigies could fill buckets. Along the paths, you see parents teaching their children to ride, their shiny little mountain bikes weaving along the track, wobbling from outrigger to outrigger. On the swings, children take turns at pushing each other, so that each can experience the thrill of flying.

Informal co-operation is going on all around us – and long may it continue to be informal. When I was a teenager, our Scout master spent one of his four weeks of annual leave taking us camping – a quarter of his annual freedom spent in a draughty tent with a load of kids. All across the country, people give up their personal time to provide new experiences or facilities for others. That indeed is selfless co-operation – and they deserve more thanks than they invariably receive.

CPD MILESTONE 134 – PERSONAL DEVELOPMENT AND THE EGO

Presence of ego is one of the benchmarks which really separates the sheep from the goats. I have a friend who spends a lot of his time travelling the world talking to groups of people about his spiritual experiences and his development path through life. When he returns from his travels and comes along to our group, it is fascinating to watch the inner ego turmoil going on. He is returning from being treated almost like a guru to becoming just one of the group again. To his credit, he usually manages to keep his ego submerged – until one of the others starts showing off his esoteric knowledge and the competitive engine threatens to kick in. But then, it's always easier to spot the ego in others than in yourself. Perhaps when I speak confidently about some subject, others see this as my ego surfacing.

CPD MILESTONE 135 – THE EGO PLACED WITHIN A MORE SELFLESS GROUP DYNAMIC

The manifestation of ego links very closely with the *belonging, assertion, co-operation* continuum that we have considered. The impact of both ego and self-confidence occurs as individuals assert active roles for themselves within the group. As each role becomes firmly established and accepted by others, however, that individual should evolve towards applying quiet confidence, with egocentric activities diminishing. As with all human dynamics, the status quo will continue to fluctuate: the more balanced the group, the more rapidly they can reduce the egocentre and integrate co-operatively.

 ## CPD MILESTONE 136 – SELFLESSNESS AND SELF-CONFIDENCE: THE POSITIVE SELF

Part of the holistic approach to life is trying to have a selfless attitude towards others; that is, interacting in such a way that you are primarily considering them rather than yourself. Helping others, perhaps by imparting detail or knowledge, boosts your self-confidence. This self-confidence is good – it makes you sound positive and look as if you are enjoying what you are doing. With many group situations, it really doesn't matter whether any one individual gains the credit, though I suppose the reckoning comes when someone else, who *is* ego-driven, claims the credit for something which you have been responsible for achieving. That's the real test of selflessness!

Before we advance to considering some of the techniques for driving our personal development forward, it's time for another Health Check.

HEALTH CHECK 4

Take some time to think about the following:

√   I can see a relationship between personal and professional development and can identify my own priorities.

√   I have thought through some of the key criteria upon which I base my life – and consider that they take account of others.

√   I am conscious of some degree of spiritual way of life which I can accept comfortably and believe that I live by its tenets.

√   I consciously try to involve myself in my local community, giving back a few of the benefits I receive in some way.

√   I am consciously trying to understand the broader issues of living a holistic way of life – and am seeking out like-minded people in order to discuss and broaden this understanding.

√   I try to respond positively to others, encouraging and helping where I can, in as selfless a way as I can currently achieve.

√   I think carefully about acts of co-operation, trying to adapt them as necessary to be as mutually effective as possible.

√   I am aware of what I consider signs of ego in others and attempt as much as possible to eliminate these in myself.

√   I can easily think of several different personal development areas which I can advance further – and am clear about possible strategies.

HOW CAN I INCREASE THE PACE OF MY PERSONAL DEVELOPMENT?

 ## CPD MILESTONE 137 – PERSONAL DEVELOPMENT AND THINKING OBJECTIVELY

I wouldn't for a moment suggest that we should formally apply cognitive processes towards developing spirituality or selflessness, such as: 'Define spirituality', 'Demonstrate an understanding of the term', 'Apply spirituality in four everyday situations', or 'Analyse the spiritual attitude encapsulated in such-and-such an action.' Flippancy aside, however, there is still a developmental sequence there which makes sense, if applied in a flexible, understanding way.

In our earlier study of objectives, we established that writing objectives and thinking objectively makes you aware of the *standards* you intend to achieve, puts you in mind of the *conditions* and encourages you to think in terms of *actions* and *outcomes*.

For personal development issues, we can probably leave the conditions to one side – and standards will be encapsulated more in our longer-term goals. This leaves thinking in terms of actions and outcomes as the most important element.

PERSONAL ACTIONS AND OUTCOMES

It's this end point which is all important: if you think in action/outcome terms, it makes the required responses much clearer. This is why it's not being a member of a committee which is important for your CPD, it's what you actively *do* on that committee. It's not the title of the course which you attended which is important, it's the outcomes which you *achieved*. It's not being interested in such-and-such a subject, it's what you've *produced* as a result of your interest.

The most powerful thing you can do to change the world,
is to change your own beliefs about the nature of life, people, reality
to something more positive ... and begin to act accordingly

Shakti Gawain, *Creative Visualization*,
Whatever Publishing Inc., 1978

 ## CPD MILESTONE 138 – THINKING IN THE ACTIVE RATHER THAN THE PASSIVE

With a bit of practice, you can get into the way of making statements in an active way. There is a key difference between expression in the active, and in the passive. It's our good friend self-ownership again. Contrast the passive statement: 'The report will be completed and forwarded by tomorrow', with a tighter, more active equivalent: 'I will complete the report and have it on your desk by noon tomorrow.'

Thinking in the active is thinking ownership and responsibility. Thinking in the first-person active means sticking a label including *your* name on the action – committing yourself to delivering the goods. Thinking in the active motivates you to get things done, not through the fear of blame but for the enjoyment of success.

Example

If I was planning how I might work on some element of my personal development – say to improve my ability to talk sociably with strangers – I might list the areas I needed to practise:

- Improve my memory retention of people's names.
- Consider opening 'ice breaker' statements.
- Plan ways of finding out the other party's interests.
- Practise making opening statements in a positive voice.
- Listen to statements to establish follow-up questions.

Although the content would have to be developed, it is evident in each of these statements what action I would have to take to become competent at these different elements. Each one makes you automatically think 'what do I have to *do* here?'

CPD MILESTONE 139 – OBJECTIVITY IN PERSONAL DEVELOPMENT

You sometimes see statements which are called objectives starting with 'understand . . .' or 'show an awareness of . . .' These are not precise enough. If I ask you to 'show an awareness of the opening statements you can make when speaking to a stranger', you can assure me that you know a few, maybe even tell me a few that you might use – and that's it: objective accomplished. But is it?

If, on the other hand, you 'practise making opening statements to someone, using a positive voice', you're not merely thinking about the types of statements you can use. You're also practising them in some form of simulated scenario, concentrating on the sound of your voice and reviewing your degree of success. There is a focus on achieving standards, so it gives you more to monitor your development against.

 ## CPD MILESTONE 140 – THINKING OBJECTIVELY AND IMPARTIALLY

Thinking objectively is not just thinking in action terms, however, it also incorporates logical, impartial thought. The Oxford English Dictionary defines 'objective', used as an adjective, as 'dealing with outward things, exhibiting actual facts uncoloured by exhibitor's feelings or opinions'. This incorporates our efforts towards being more selfless; discussing matters without being judgemental and remaining calm, however nervous or unsettled we might feel below the surface. Combine the different elements together and we finish up with measured progress, effective actions and considerate involvement with others.

> *Do not be desirous of having things done quickly.*
> *Do not look at small advantages.*
> *Desire to have things done quickly prevents their being done*
>   *thoroughly.*
> *Looking at small advantages prevents great affairs from being*
>   *accomplished.*
>
>   Confucius

CPD MILESTONE 141 – PERSONAL DEVELOPMENT AND CPD PLANNING AND RECORDING

Thinking in objective, active terms and using a CPD structure such as we have been discussing, we can plan our personal activities and goals in much the same way as we do our professional ones.

Consider the following personal development objectives:

○ As school board member, sub-committee chair, I will produce the five policy statements identified in the development plan and update the school prospectus.
○ As hall committee secretary, I will organize the appeal for new building funds, in order to achieve donations of at least £4000.
○ I will write at least three articles for publishing, including one which will be aimed at a publication style which differs from those to which I normally submit copy.
○ I will communicate positively with friends and neighbours, providing encouragement and advice where required and assisting them where they consider this to be beneficial. I will record such incidents in order to monitor my activity rather than to boost my ego.

If you look at these examples, you will see that they are all stated in action terms. As with business objectives, if you consider the content and implications of each statement, you should see how the activity breaks down into a progressive sequence of actions.

CPD MILESTONE 142 – SETTING OUT OUR PERSONAL MILESTONES

This analysis gives us the milestones needed to identify progress, and some idea of the techniques and activities necessary for us to ultimately reach our stated goal. Establishing these milestones will give us the stages along our personal path where we can record progress in our CPD record, always bearing in mind that this is a fairly mechanistic logging of steps in what is in effect a continuous, ongoing development.

CPD MILESTONE 143 – THE EVER-EXPANDING STATE OF PERSONAL DEVELOPMENT

Although I can log completion of the policy statements as a milestone of achievement in my stated governor role, the quality, frequency and complexity of our good deeds done for neighbours and community should just grow and grow – each action is perhaps finite but there is no ultimate end point (apart from death!).

Individuals are thus engaged in personal development activities which intermingle both with their own professional development activities and the overall development activities of others in their relationship group. As progress in personal development encourages individuals to take a more holistic attitude towards relationships with others, the atmosphere of group co-operation should gradually flourish. This can of course take time and will undoubtedly be slower than we would desire.

ESTABLISHING ACCEPTABLE PERSONAL DEVELOPMENT OUTCOMES

It is harder to specifically record personal development outcomes which are 'good works', rather than competency achievement. The whole concept of continuous personal development is still quite new, and there is certainly a need for dialogue to establish parameters, areas for inclusion and degrees of acceptability. Certainly, work within the community at informal as well as formal levels is a valuable vehicle for development – and an effective CPD planning/recording system must provide a broad scope for recording such activities and outcomes, in order that progress is charted as precisely and developmentally as possible.

CONCLUSION

We have seen that personal development within the community will give us broader experience of working with others. Applying our evolving selfless, objective and ego-free thinking within the group will improve this co-operative atmosphere even further. With appropriate mentoring and guidance, linked with the synergy of like-minded souls acting in unison, there is no reason why the co-operative atmosphere cannot flourish.

CPD MILESTONE 144 – MAINTAINING OUR INDIVIDUAL MOMENTUM

Personal development is thus ongoing. It integrates with professional development – but moves at a different rate. Take an alternative therapy, such as massage, for example. A trained practitioner can use all the prescribed techniques and actions, but as the receiving body, you may feel that they are just 'going through the motions', without much rapport. If the masseur has developed an awareness of and link with the receiving body, there is a more intense flow and meaning to the actions, as they react more deeply with the physical and psychological needs of the body. Thus, the advance in personal development has improved the professional outcome.

 ## CPD MILESTONE 145 – ESTABLISHING THE GROUND RULES FOR A HOLISTIC LIFE

Each individual will have his or her own priorities and criteria upon which to build personal development tenets. These will vary between individuals, with some seeing this form of development as secondary to the key issue of job and wage improvement. Some will continue to see it as totally unimportant, or impossible to apply to any degree within a business context. What is important is that it feels right to you at the time – I would never force anyone towards development activities which they did not feel comfortable at attempting. When you feel that the time is appropriate, then you can give thought to some of the options open to you.

TWENTY TENETS FOR A MORE HOLISTIC WAY OF LIFE

- ○ Build positive thought.
- ○ Be aware of yourself and others.
- ○ Believe in yourself and others.
- ○ Act as selflessly as you can.
- ○ Allow time to do things properly.
- ○ Give matters time to evolve.
- ○ Allow yourself 'Time Out' for thinking.
- ○ Rest, relax and focus (meditate).
- ○ Use visualization to concentrate thought.
- ○ Observe and learn from world affairs.
- ○ Work towards co-operation and away from egocentricity.
- ○ Consider the effects of your actions.
- ○ Apply holistic thinking when the time seems appropriate.
- ○ Do what ultimately feels right.
- ○ Reduce your dependence on stimulants and medication.
- ○ Believe in the healing power of positive thought.
- ○ Exercise in as natural an environment as possible.
- ○ Retain an overview of the Bigger Picture.
- ○ Maintain a flexible view of your development path.
- ○ Amend your plans openly to maintain progress.

There's enough there to keep you going for the rest of your life . . . and beyond! Give it some thought – and action – when YOU feel the time is right.

DISTANT HILLS – CHARTED PATHS

We have considered a lot of information since we set out on our meandering journey along the long straight track of Continuing Personal and Professional Development. If you have managed to consider the CPD Milestones we have passed this far – and perhaps been able to apply some of them in developing individuals', as well as your own, needs – you will be clear about many of the outcomes.

You will also be more aware of the recurring strengths and shortfalls, the personal and professional development priorities which you have mutually established with others, and the range of techniques and methods which you might apply. Perhaps, as a DSF staff member or as a mentor, you have tested this thinking within the three corners of the integrated triangle.

 ## CPD MILESTONE 146 – CPD PLANNING AND RECORDING

Having selected planning methods for at least some of these CPD activities, you will have applied objective thinking to the process and can think in terms of actions and planned outcomes. You will have seen the benefit of using some form of documented system, in order to maintain an overview of the CPD plans – and record their completion. You'll also be aware that any system must respond flexibly to individual needs – as servant rather than master – making its completion a helpful support rather than a tedious chore.

You'll be aware of how individual CPD systems can be used positively for related purposes by everyone within the integrated triangle, and understand that this triangle provides flexible support, which can be reviewed and adapted regularly to respond to changing needs and conditions.

APPROACHING TIME FLEXIBLY

You will also be conscious that the key element over which you may have little control is the overall time it takes any individual to progress from A to B to C along the path, but you'll know how to regularly review the timing and route positively, creating additional remedial milestones where required, to maintain motivation and momentum.

In short, if you can sense the benefits of empowerment within a holistic, co-operative atmosphere, you will be supportive of the need for individuals to take responsibility for their development – both personal and professional. You'll also be more aware that these two areas of development, though in some ways separate, can work in close harmony with each other, building towards more integrated outcomes. This deeper awareness is a key tenet of the holistic principle.

You'll also understand the benefits of working within the energy of the integrated triangle, at any one time either as DSF member, mentor or individual learner. You may already have experienced some or all of these roles. The triangle is flexible, the learning process a fluid continuum, the outcomes beneficial to all parties.

CPD MILESTONE 147 – REVIEWING THE BIGGER PICTURE

Having a view of the bigger picture from an elevated perspective, you can see the future progress of the development paths over which you hold some watching brief – including your own path. Through this overview, you appreciate the need for an open, flexible approach towards maintaining progress along the way ahead. You can also acknowledge the importance of reviewing and updating goals and objectives regularly, to ensure that development progresses in line with the future needs of each individual, his/her/your current and prospective employers . . . and society in general.

Charting the development path – that is, establishing and maintaining active plans, recording progress and reviewing future needs – becomes the basis for an effective continuing personal and professional development (CPD) system.

CPD MILESTONE 148 – REVIEWING OUR GOALS

We have established the importance of thinking in an objective way – focusing on activities and outcomes, while keeping a reference view of the standards required to hand. By thinking in the linear, developmental way encouraged by the *cognitive* sequence, you are aware of the benefits of both planning activities following this line of development, and the need to consolidate the new learning through work-related reinforcement. Using the objective structure when writing your goals and establishing your milestones will help you think actively, thus maintaining the momentum. It will also help you spot blockages as they arise and make any necessary amendments.

Consider the following, as they apply to yourself as individual learner:

○ I am aware of my own strengths and shortfalls.
○ I have translated these into my personal and professional development needs.
○ I have prioritized these against my own developmental plans.
○ I have reviewed this priority against work and other external requirements.
○ I have established the sequence of milestones which I plan to follow.
○ I have discussed methods and techniques of achieving these milestones.
○ I am aware of how the individual/mentor/DSF triangle integrates positively.
○ I have selected formats for planning and monitoring my activities.
○ I have used these to write down strategies for my planned goals.
○ I am ready to start on this path – or have already started.

That's how the whole process maps out when you apply it to your own needs and priorities. It works in the same way for any individual, of course, when you are functioning in the role of mentor or DSF staff member. Whether for yourself or someone else, it's all the same – only the motivation and involvement is different; not *less*, but different!

 ## CPD MILESTONE 149 – KEEPING AN OPEN MIND

We cannot expect too much too quickly. The concepts we have been considering represent a fairly radical shift to many and will take time to establish. It is also likely that companies – and individuals – will be keener to apply some aspects than others. I'm a strong believer in learning to walk properly before we run, as long as we ensure that the walking experience is positive and successful. It's that old cognitive sequence again! We select conditions, subjects and participants in order to best ensure this positive success.

WHAT YOU *SAY* IS WHAT YOU GET

We must, of course, maintain an open mind regarding the expectations we can place on others but, where the integrated triangle concept is functioning positively, reference to the procedures and structures we have considered will make our requests more precise. If people know clearly what someone wants, they are more likely to help them get it!

MAKING THE SYSTEM WORK

The system is most likely to work in a department where managers are keen on the concepts of mentoring and empowered individuals. The DSF development support will work best where the facilities and staff are made available. Being realistic, if the concept is a success to any great degree, the DSF may have difficulty keeping abreast of the increasing pace. Similarly, we must ensure that the demands made on internal mentoring do not place too heavy a burden on day-to-day work priorities.

One step at a time, on tried and tested footholds

However, this is not a hesitant response – it's the reasoning behind moving from small beginnings towards greater successes. These, in turn, can then be used as stepping stones for yet further development. I have worked with many companies who were making the first tentative steps from the known territory of delivered courses into the new fields of open and distance learning. It certainly requires a different attitude – and a greater belief in self-empowerment – but many of them have made the transition successfully ... and are benefiting from the experience.

CPD MILESTONE 150 – EMPOWERMENT – TAKING THE LEAD WILLINGLY

We have been considering and applying mentoring and the revised DSF role throughout the book, without having chapters specifically on 'How to train a mentor' or 'Changing a Training Department into a Development Support Function'. This is not an omission but a conscious application of my strong belief in self-empowerment. The information necessary is all within this book: objective structuring, the developing learning sequence, the progression towards co-operation, the range of techniques, the flexible response towards the individual, and so on. The raw material is there; you have the ability. The particular needs of your environment need thought and planning – leading towards decision and action. Work as a team, think it through – go for it! Below are a few pointers, to help you progress.

CONSIDER THIS: MENTORING

○   The most important prerequisite is a patient, supportive attitude.
○   Information should be given in 'bite-sized chunks', with added consolidation.
○   Mentors must be aware of the sequencing of learning – and apply it.
○   Development will combine the benefits of both informality and structure.
○   The differences between mentoring, coaching and delivery must be clearly seen.

CONSIDER THIS: DEVELOPING A DSF

○   This involves an attitude shift from reactive to proactive.
○   Learning and development must be considered in short, flexible modules.
○   The priority is providing learning to the individual, not individuals for the learning.
○   It requires the use of the widest range of learning techniques and resources possible.
○   The integrated approach requires an easy-to-use CPD planning and recording system.

CPD MILESTONE 151 – INDIVIDUAL DEVELOPMENT PATHS (OR LIFE AS A BOWL OF SPAGHETTI)

We must keep an open mind regarding the planning and implementation of individual development paths. Retain the mental picture of the intertwining strands, like spaghetti, which constitute these paths, each with a little figure at its leading end. Each figure may double back, waver to the sides or indeed remain static for periods. However good our planning and 'defensive thinking', we must accept the fact that situations will arise where new strategies must be considered, certain activities put on hold or overlying decisions made which may affect individual priorities dramatically. It is important to plan – it gives us the 'intended' against which to compare the 'actual' – but we must plan realistically, and retain a flexible view on life.

CPD MILESTONE 152 – INTEGRATING WITH OTHERS

There are probably three overriding messages which I hope to have given clearly:

○ first, the value of objective thinking when applied in so many different ways;
○ second, the flexible continuum of the integrated triangle, and
○ third, the importance of the belonging/assertion/co-operation progression.

If, as a group, we can consciously strive towards living and working together more co-operatively, much stress, delay and anger can simply disappear. Whether the team is a family, an activity or sports team, a works department, a nation or beyond, matters not – the principle remains the same. The old business paradigm says that this is nonsense: 'they're all lazy bastards and you can't trust them.' The new business paradigm asks 'how do you like to be treated?' 'Fine – well, treat others the same way and everyone will benefit.' In other words, *do unto others as you would that they should do unto you* – simple, really!

The response won't be universal – there's a lot of fat-cat, self-centred greed around – but large movements can result from small beginnings, when ever-increasing numbers of people co-operate. Try being the first tall poppy, or the first of the hundred monkeys!

People have always progressed – and will continue to do so – at different individual rates. When climbing, it is normal to overtake someone without using their head as a foothold. It is even feasible to point out some good moves for them to take, to speed their progress up the rockface. It is not necessary to discredit others in order to cement your own progress; it is equally not necessary to undermine the views of others in order to promote your own. Where necessary, meet assertion with assertion to allow both to then progress towards co-operation. But with clear goals and a planned CPD path, you can progress along the track in harmony with others.

THE FOUR-WAY TEST

In 1998, my wife and I had a wonderful holiday in Malaysia and Sumatra, facilitated brilliantly by a guide called Resham Singh. On the final day, in Penang, we hired a taxi to take us round a wide range of Buddhist and Chinese temples. Our conversation with the driver turned to matters spiritual and alternative therapies and he told us about a reflexology path in the municipal park. As you probably know, a reflexologist manipulates the pressure points in your hands and feet to improve the overall well-being of your body. A human therapist, yes . . . but I'd never heard of a reflexology path!

This turned out to be a winding path constructed from sea-smoothed pebbles mounted on edge in cement. Walking barefoot along this path was at the same time both very painful and strangely releasing. By the side of this path was a sign in English:

THE FOUR-WAY TEST

FOR THE THINGS WE THINK, SAY OR DO –

1. IS IT THE TRUTH?
2. IS IT FAIR TO ALL CONCERNED?
3. WILL IT BUILD GOODWILL AND BETTER FRIENDSHIPS?
4. WILL IT BE BENEFICIAL TO ALL CONCERNED?

This, remember, was in a public park in a Malaysian town, provided for locals rather than tourists. Can you imagine a similar sign placed in London's Hyde Park, and remaining there without being covered with graffiti?

Perhaps the West hasn't progressed quite so far or in as correct a direction as we like to believe. Perhaps it's time to stop the spin and re-examine the underlying truths.

CPD MILESTONE 153 – ONWARDS AND UPWARDS

The concept of the integrated triangle, incorporating individual, manager/mentor and Development Support Function will flourish where it is built on strong foundations and is given the support of a flexible CPD system which is designed and maintained to meet the needs of each developing individual. This integrated approach, building progressively in a co-operative manner, will lead more and more towards a holistic outcome – with the overall effect to all those concerned greater than the sum of the individual elements.

Continuing Personal and Professional Development thus becomes much more than merely keeping a record of activities, to being an overall system or philosophy, where the initials CPD will also stand for:

○   **Complete Proficiency Diagnosis**
○   **Carefully Prepared Design**
○   **Comprehensive Personal Documentation**
○   **Compromise Progress Definition**
○   **Complementary Practicals and Discussions,** and
○   **Complete Programme Delivery.**

. . . no longer a pile of paperwork, more a holistic way of life!

90 Brain Teasers for Trainers

Graham Roberts-Phelps and Anne McDougall

The activities and exercises in this collection are designed to broaden perception, and improve learning, thinking and problem-solving skills. Using them is also a valuable way to boost energy levels at the beginning, middle or end of any training session.

The collection will help any group engage all five senses in their learning, and develop creative and lateral thinking, word usage, mental dexterity and cooperative team skills. Most of the activities require no more than a flip chart or OHP to run. And because they need only a few moments preparation, they can be planned into sessions in advance, or simply introduced to fill gaps, or to signal a change of direction, as appropriate.

Trainers, teachers and team leaders will find *Brain Teasers for Trainers* a rich source of simple, flexible, and easy-to-use exercises, as well as the inspiration for their own variants.

Gower

Gower Handbook of Training and Development

Third Edition

Edited by Anthony Landale

It is now crystal clear that, in today's ever-changing world, an organization's very survival depends upon how it supports its people to learn and keep on learning. Of course this new imperative has considerable implications for trainers who are now playing an increasingly critical role in supporting individuals, teams and business management. In this respect today's trainers may need to be more than excellent presenters; they are also likely to require a range of consultancy and coaching skills, to understand the place of technology in supporting learning and be able to align personal development values with business objectives.

This brand new edition of the *Gower Handbook of Training and Development* will be an invaluable aid for today's training professional as they face up to the organizational challenges presented to them. All 38 chapters in this edition are new and many of the contributors, whilst being best-selling authors or established industry figures, are appearing for the first time in this form. Edited by Anthony Landale, this *Handbook* builds on the foundations that previous editions have laid down whilst, at the same time, highlighting many of the very latest advances in the industry.

The *Handbook* is divided into five sections - learning organization, best practice, advanced techniques in training and development, the use of IT in learning, and evaluation issues.

Gower

Handbook of Management Games and Simulations

Sixth Edition

Edited by Chris Elgood

What kinds of management games are there? How do they compare with other methods of learning? Where can I find the most suitable games for the training objectives I have in mind?

Handbook of Management Games and Simulations provides detailed answers to these questions and many others.

Part 1 of the *Handbook* examines the characteristics and applications of the different types of game. It explains how they promote learning and the circumstances for which they are best suited.

Part 2 comprises a detailed directory of some 300 games and simulations. Each one is described in terms of its target group, subject area, nature and purpose, and the means by which the outcome is established and made known. The entries also contain administrative data including the number of players, the number of teams and the time required. Several indexes enable readers to locate precisely those games that would be relevant for their own needs.

This sixth edition has been revised to reflect recent developments. And of course the directory has been completely updated. Chris Elgood's *Handbook* will continue to be indispensable for anyone concerned with management development.

Gower

The Mentoring Manual

Mike Whittaker and Ann Cartwright

A good mentoring scheme can have a transformational effect on both the people it is designed to help (the mentees) and those providing the help (the mentors). But, as with other work-based development processes, it needs commitment, reflection, planning and resources to make the scheme work.

The Mentoring Manual reflects many of the prerequisites for a successful mentoring scheme and qualities of an effective mentor:

• Exceptional breadth of experience - wide-ranging examples from businesses, the voluntary sector, higher and secondary education
• Access to new ideas and best practice - alongside the ideas and examples, there are forms, questions, exercises and other photocopiable materials for the trainer or facilitator
• A belief in enabling people to develop their own solutions - this isn't a blueprint for you to pick up and follow, rather a series of signposts that you can follow or ignore in developing your own scheme
• A recognition of the value of a holistic approach - there's help here on understanding mentoring, planning and designing a scheme, selling the concept to others, launching and sustaining the scheme, developing mentors and mentees, as well as reviewing the success of what you are doing
• A language that people can understand - the style and the structure of the book make it very easy to find your way around. This is a book for someone who really wants to know how to make a success of their mentoring scheme ... starting today.

Mike Whittaker and Ann Cartwright provide you with the enthusiasm, the theory and practical materials for starting a new scheme or revitalizing an existing one. They will also help you to win over the decision makers, recruit mentors and mentees and develop champions for the mentoring cause.

You need to provide the commitment to the mentoring process along with an openness to new ideas. *The Mentoring Manual* will provide a catalyst for practically everything else.

Gower

Successful Communication Through NLP

A Trainer's Guide

Sally Dimmick

Most professional trainers nowadays have some understanding of Neuro Linguistic Programming. They probably know that people take in information about the world through a 'preferred representational channel' and that we communicate better with people if we use their preferred channel - visual, auditory or kinaesthetic. Sally Dimmick's book goes further. It shows how NLP principles can be applied to every aspect of training and which particular aids and methods are the most suitable for each channel.

The first part of the text outlines the main concepts of NLP and explains how to identify a person's preferred channel. It also looks briefly at the significance of learning styles. Part II examines each representational channel in turn and relates it to the corresponding training methods and materials. The final chapter provides ways of combining the channels so as to maximize the transfer of learning. The text is enlivened throughout by anecdotes, examples and illustrations.

For teachers, trainers, managers and indeed anyone faced with the need to communicate in a professional way, Sally Dimmick's guide will prove invaluable. It will be particularly welcomed by trainers looking for practical advice on how to use NLP.

Gower